The Travelogue of a Lost Girl

No-one is truly lost, they are simply adapting to their habitat

The Travelogue of a Lost Girl

No-one is truly lost, they are simply adapting to their habitat

By

VISHNUPRIYA PILLAI

Book Title: The Travelogue of a Lost Girl
Written and Illustrated by: Vishnupriya Pillai
Print and Distribution Partners: Amazon, Notion Press, Flipkart

Publisher: Kerala Publishers, Trivandrum, Kerala, India - 695009
E-mail: publish@keralapublishers.com
Website: www.keralapublishers.com

ISBN: 979-8-89186-260-9

First Printing: November 2023
Cover Illustration: Karthik Gopinath
Copy Editing and Typeset By: Accent Premedia Group
Website: www.accentpremedia.com

CONTENTS

ABOUT THE BOOK

I'm pretty sure most folks reading this book are like me – people who've spent their whole lives in a place that's not where their roots lie. We live in a land where almost everyone's an immigrant, and we only make a quick stopover in our homeland once or twice a year. But each time we go back, it feels like we're on a brand-new adventure. Why? Because we're not the same person we were the last time we visited, and every return brings fresh experiences our way.

That's the essence of this book, really. Most travel stories are about exploring far-off, exotic places. But here, we're celebrating the beauty of returning to a familiar spot. Even if it's a tiny, hidden village in a small state in a massive country, you'd be amazed at how much there is to discover, learn, and experience, year after year. You see, each visit transforms you a little bit, and so you come back to your old stomping grounds with new stories to tell and fresh adventures to live. It's a continuous cycle of rediscovery and growth that makes every homecoming feel like a brand-new journey.

DEDICATION

*My Appuppan, Ammumma, Manu Maman,
Chinnu Maami, Ambadi and all those who
made my vacation a memorable one.*

INTRODUCTION

Here is the thing about traveling to your hometown which you only visit once a year. It's like hitting a reset button on life. Every time I step foot in Kerala, it's like a vacation mode is automatically activated. I get to soak in the rain, feel the breeze, and feast my eyes on the stunning Kerala scenery. Plus, the best part is, I can kiss my school drama studies goodbye for a while. Talk about pure relaxation!

But here is the annoying part. I also have to deal with an army of annoying bugs—ants, beetles, praying mantises, spiders, you name it. These little terrors love to give me tiny, itchy bumps that I can't help but scratch, even though I know it'll make them grow bigger. Ugh, it's a real bummer.

That's why I decided to document my experiences in Kerala, so be ready to experience a life-changing adventure (well, not really) of the ups and downs and hilarious moments of me and my family.

DAY 0 – AIRPORT DISASTER

I don't know about you, but when I am going somewhere, I am always way too prepared. I pack my suitcases 5 days before. WHY? Because I'm so excited that I want to shove my excitement on something.

So, when my sister and mother were packing, I had nothing to do because I already packed. And the worst thing was that I needed to put new clothes on. I had to dig through that suitcase and then put my clothes on. It was such a HASSLE.

Then, on the day of the flight to India, something weird happened. I woke up, and out of the blue, my vision started going all blurry. This wasn't the first time it had happened. I'd experienced it before during a test at school, and it gave me a killer headache. I can't remember what happened next, but I figured it would pass just like last time. So, I splashed my face with water, but nope, the blurriness stuck around, like that one annoying pimple.

So I did the logical thing and went to go tell my sister (SPOILER ALERT it was not logical), and she made it sound like a big deal to my mom. Now, my mom's convinced I'm going blind and starts Googling like crazy. Meanwhile, I get hit by this monster headache, like a wrecking ball smacked my noggin. It felt like someone was scraping my head with a needle. Ouch! My dad comes back and tells me to pop some pills. I start popping Panadol like candy, but it doesn't help much. We're supposed to leave in 30 minutes, so I try to get ready, but I can barely move. Then, suddenly, I gotta hurl, and I'm puking like there's no tomorrow. Nasty, right? But, strangely enough, after puking my guts out, I actually feel better, even though my mouth tastes like vomit.

Which is literally the worst feeling in the world because no matter what you do, it just sticks, and your breath will smell bad too. But I didn't want to go brush my teeth. It's a struggle for me to do it once a day. I am not doing it twice.

But my mom's still convinced I might puke again, so she stuffs some tissue papers and some plastic bags into my bag, and we rush to the airport. In the car, I've got motion sickness, which is totally normal for me, so I try to snooze it off. But after about 15 minutes, we reach the airport, and I hop out. It's one of those "uh-oh, I messed up" moments because, yep, I puke again, this time into the plastic bag my mom gave me. I feel awful, and the last thing I want to do is get on a plane.

But obviously we get through the check-in, weigh our bags, and I'm finally feeling relieved. No headache, no nausea. But then obviously something good can't last more than 5 seconds for me, and we found out that the weight of our bags was WAY more than expected, and we have to ditch some fruits from our luggage into my backpack. My mom's mad as a hornet. I'm still not feeling great, so my sis has to carry the fruits, and now she's mad too. To sum it up, everyone is angry, and honestly, I don't think anyone is beaming while walking through an airport. Even babies, who are always happy, cry in an airport.

We went through security, reached the final exit, and all we need to do is grab some food and hop on the plane.

So, my sis went to grab some McDonald's for everyone, but just as she's about to get it, I felt queasy again and dashed to the nearest bathroom. Oddly enough, nothing happened. But while that was going on I didn't realize that my mom was following me the entire time so since my mom comes with me, and someone has taken our seats. My sis started yelling for my mom,

"WHERE ARE YOU?!" After dealing with my sister's hollering, we finally regrouped, but all the seats were taken. We asked this nice lady if we can share her table, and she's cool with it.

My sis went to a nearby clinic to fetch some meds, and I gobbled down a hamburger. Then, I swallowed a pill. No one's hungry, so we headed to the gate. On the way, I spotted a washroom, and that triggered it. I puked in a stall, and it felt odd not to have someone patting my back. But guess what? I felt loads better, even though I knew it's gross. The weird part was, I puked after taking the medicine, so my sis had to check with the pharmacist at the clinic. He said the medicine probably got into my bloodstream, so I dodged a bullet there. But I'm done with vomiting; if there was a "no vomit" button, I'd hit it.

My sister literally did everything for us until this point so she's furious. We finally made it to the gate. My mom had our passports and boarding passes, but my sis and I were way ahead of her. Every time we reached a checkpoint, we looked back at my mom, and she's clueless, smiling at everyone like she's at a party. When she caught up, she's like, "What's going on?" We just say, "Passport," and she hands it to the officer.

Finally, we boarded the plane, and things seemed fine. But guess what? I couldn't sleep, no matter how hard I tried. I fidgeted and twisted in my seat for hours. It's torture. I checked my phone like a gazillion times, and my mom thought using a phone on a plane will make it explode.

When we finally landed in India, the plane's shaking, and then I realized we reached Kerala not the airport yet. I waited until I felt the plane descending, and then it hits me—I was so stoked to get off this flight.

When we slowly got out of the plane the first thing, I noticed was that in India there was no bus to take you off the plane instead there was a connecting shaft. We cleared security, and

I spotted a teacher who works at my school. I recognized her, but I was not sure if she remembers me, so I didn't say hi. My mom got wind of this and thought I was being rude.

Later, we found out that the teacher was eyeballing me the whole time, or at least that's what my sister thought. So maybe she did remember me, and I felt kinda bad for not saying hi. We also met my school mates Aysha and Asiya, the twins and one of my mom's seniors from her college at the passport verification queue.

We grabbed our bags, and my sis and I did all the heavy lifting. When we finally got outside, we couldn't find my uncle. We kept searching until we spotted him hiding with my aunt and cousin. I couldn't remember the last time I saw them, but they looked the same. My aunt was thrilled to see us, and so far I'm loving the idea of spending a month here.

Oh! I forgot to tell you where I am going to spend my vacation. It's my mom's native place called Kottukkal, located in the Ittiva Grama Panchayath in the Kollam district of the southern Indian state of Kerala. It is situated in the southwestern part of India, specifically in the southwestern region of the Indian subcontinent.

It is widely believed that the name "Kottukkal" could be derived from the Malayalam word "Kottu," which means "fort," and "Kal," which means "stone" or "rock." This suggests that the name may refer to the presence of forts or rocky formations in the area. Indeed, it is! Kottukkal Rock temple (Cave temple) is a quite famous heritage site.

It was expected to be a half-hour drive to Kottukkal from Thiruvananthapuram International Airport, and I was kind of worried about traffic, but guess what? It was super early, and there was no traffic at all! Lucky us!

As we drove, I stared out the window. Kottukkal is like a magical place right out of a storybook. It is a hilly area, and the air is so crisp and cool. It feels like a different world compared to UAE where we live.

Our house in Kottukkal is awesome! It is surrounded by a rubber plantation. Imagine living in a forest of rubber trees! It is like living in a real-life jungle!

What makes our location particularly unique is that our house is nestled right amid a temple, church, and mosque, the sacred places of worship, creating a harmonious and spiritually enriched environment.

I saw my Appuppan and Ammumma (grandpa and grandma) waiting for us in the sit out, and it's been ages since I saw them. We hugged, and it's all warm and fuzzy. Next thing I knew, I was up in the movie room with my mom and sis, lying down, and then I was out like a light in seconds.

DAY 1 – VELLAPOKKAM (FLOOD)

In all the years I have lived (12 years which is a lot of experience on my resume), I never thought that I would encounter a flood in my house, which is something that I find pretty ironic. When I first reached India, my only wish was that it would rain, but sadly once I reached, I realized that it hadn't rained for the past weekend and wasn't going to rain anytime soon.

So, when I finally woke up, I noticed a couple of things I missed the previous day because, you know, I was dead tired. First off, they decided to switch up the bedroom setup. Now, the bed was all the way on the opposite side of the room, far away from the dinky TV. It used to be right next to the TV, so it was kinda weird.

But what really caught my attention was the fact that there was no one in the room anymore. So, I dragged myself downstairs, and there were my mom and sis, sprawled out on the couch, practically napping. Today was my aunt's day off, so my mom was giving her the lowdown on our life in the UAE. Looking back, it was quite entertaining, and honestly, it turned out to be the highlight of the day.

Later on, when my cousin Ambadi got back from school, he decided to take his bicycle for a spin in our front yard. My mom was absolutely mesmerized as he showed off his two "awesome" tricks: standing up while riding. By the way, I could do that too, but my mom had never seen it before, so she was all impressed.

Then, out of the blue, she turned to me and asked, "Don't you know how to cycle?"

I replied, "Yeah, I do."

And she said with the straightest face on: "You know you're really short right now; you should go cycle, you might grow taller."

Challenge accepted! I ignored the not-so-subtle jab and hopped on the bicycle. Just as I was getting all set, my sister accidentally made a noise, and my mom shifted her focus.

"Can you ride a bicycle?" She asked my sister.

My sis hesitated and said, "No."

And that's when it all went downhill for my sister. My mom won't let it slide until my sis gets on the darn bicycle. So, I quickly got off and said, "It's all yours" to my sis with a sly grin.

She got on, started complaining about not having enough space and the cycle being too big. In the midst of her protests, she lost balance and catapulted herself, smacking into an innocent pipe, breaking the tap and unleashing a waterfall in our driveway.

In panic mode, my grandfather rushed to shut off the water supply to the house, and we eventually fixed the pipe. But not before my cousin, feeling brave, hopped back on the bike, only to slip on the water-slicked ground and went face-first. It was at this moment that I realized I was the only one who hadn't goofed up today. I'm practically perfect, so I obviously bragged about it to my dad during our daily video call.

Little did we know that our problems were far from over. When my cousin went upstairs to take a bath, he discovered that there's no water. And this was after the pipe got fixed so we turned the water supply back on. So, he investigated and found the entire floor flooded—it was basically a pond. If we couldn't get all the water out, at least we could've started breeding fish in there.

Naturally, we did alert the whole house and called our uncle for help. Meanwhile, we're on a hunt to figure out where the water's coming from. Turned out, it's gushing out from a screw behind the TV.

Help arrived, and it turned out when the tap broke and we stopped the water, one of the old tanks exploded, punching *a hole in the wall, and all the water flowed into the room. Who knew that could even happen? After going up and down to check on the tank, we managed to stop the water, but of course, one problem leads to another.*

Now it's our job to clear all the water from the room, armed with just a squeegee, a bucket, and a tray—you know the best tools to exist on this planet. The grown-ups decided it's on us because my sister kinda started this mess. So, thank you.

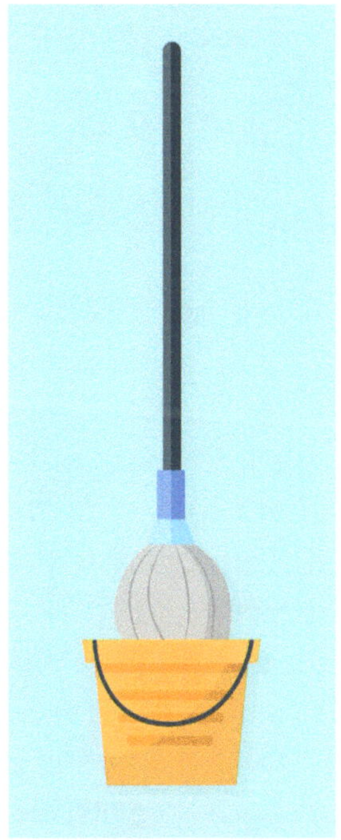

There's only one door to the backyard, and it did fully open. As we're trying to get the water out, we're basically splashing it all over ourselves. My cousin got soaked, my sis refused to touch the water and just inches along with the squeegee while perched on the couch, even though it's her fault. And the whole time, I was yelling, "CHILD ABUSE!"

It's a sad fate, really. That was the room where my mom, sis, and I were supposed to sleep, but it smelled so bad that it was impossible. So, I ended up crashing on the living room couch, where I tossed and turned all night. That sofa was impossible to sleep on, 'cause I couldn't fully stretch my legs. So, all I could do was fidget and try different positions. Eventually, I gave up and asked my mom to switch with me, but where she's sleeping was even worse. I tried to snag a pillow from my grandpa, but he's stingy with his pillows, and he handed me one still in its plastic cover, instructing me not to take it off. So, it's like sleeping on a cloud wrapped in plastic—not exactly comfy. I switched with my mom again, and she's not too thrilled. In conclusion, it's an absolute mess, and I barely got any sleep that night.

DAY 2 – OOPS

When I finally managed to drag myself out of bed, I was seriously wiped out. I could have easily slipped back into dreamland, but the commotion around me kept me awake. Turns out, since our little room-flooding incident, my appup-pan (grandpa) had gone all Hulk and cleaned up the entire mess. By the time the rest of us woke up, it was game over; he was officially too mad at us. To make matters worse, he found some pot filled with what he thought were mosquitoes' eggs and had thrown it out pronto.

However, he hadn't cleared all the water completely, so guess whose responsibility it was to mop up the remaining dirty water and gunk from the ground? Yep, you guessed it – ours. And all we had at our disposal was one grimy mop and a mea-sly old wiper.

At first, I tried to persuade my sister to take on the mop duty, but she kept turning me down. After a while, she lost her cool and declared that I had no clue how to clean, then stormed out. Later, she had the nerve to return to the room and blast YouTube videos at max volume. Well, that was my cue to leave, and I could hear her screaming her lungs out all the way downstairs:

"YOU'LL REGRET THIS!"

"DON'T YOU DARE TAKE ONE MORE STEP!"

"COME BACK!"

When I finally reached the lower level, my mom asked if I had finished the cleaning. I awkwardly explained the situation, how my sister and I were like oil and water. My mom wasn't too thrilled and came up with a plan.

She said, "You two obviously can't function together, so here's the deal: she cleans the room, and you clean the yard."

Sounds simple, right? Wrong. What she meant was, I had to sweep up all the fallen leaves in the yard using a busted broom. And let me tell you, this yard was colossal, way too big for me to handle. I've said it before, and I'll say it again, this was basically CHILD ABUSE.

As I battled the leaves, I accidentally struck an anthill. The tiny ants swarmed my broom, furious and determined to defend their home. When I complained to my mom, she simply brushed it off.

Despite the pain in my back, I continued sweeping, and to my surprise, I finished before my sister did, earning me a brief moment of well-deserved rest.

Later, when my cousin got back from school, he dashed upstairs, searching for something. He returned looking all puzzled and asked my mom about a steel pot that was up on the balcony near the movie room. That's when it hit us: those so-called mosquito eggs were actually a mother fish and her newborn children! And just like that, my grandpa became the unintentional killer of a fishy family. There was nothing we could do, my cousin made a big fuss about that, so my grandpa promised to buy an aquarium later (which, SPOILER ALERT, never happened).

To cap off the day, I was forced to study social studies (sst), and after that ordeal, we all decided it was time to call it a night.

DAY 3 – BLIND AS A BAT

Alright, let's rewind to this totally random morning when I had a school check-up. It was your typical routine stuff – they checked my eyesight, blood pressure, height, and weight, and then we had a quick consultation. But here's where things got interesting.

So, I rocked up for the eye test, and boom, I could barely see anything! It was like a wave of confusion smacked me right in the face. I couldn't read past the second line with my left eye. But guess what? The doctor didn't say a word about it, so I thought, "Eh, maybe it's nothing."

Fast forward to when I got home. I casually told my mom about my eye-test adventure, more as a joke than anything else. Now, you need to know something about my mom. When you tell her something, she doesn't just leave it there. She lets it simmer in her brain for days, maybe even weeks, and then she drops her verdict. So, a week later, I overheard her telling my dad that she thinks (read KNOW) I need glasses.

Next thing I know, we're in India, and without even consulting my non-consenting self, she's booked an eye appointment for me. Oh, the joy! She woke me up at the crack of 9 a.m., which might not sound crazy early, but consider that my body clock was still on UAE time, so it was more like 7:30 a.m. for me. I got dressed, hopped into an auto-rickshaw with my mom, and off we went to the clinic. Throughout the ride, I stubbornly clung to my belief that my eyes were perfectly fine, thank you very much. My mom, on the other hand, seemed convinced otherwise, citing our family history of glasses-wearing – my dad with his shortsightedness, mom with her longsightedness, and my sister with both shortsightedness and astigmatism.

Now, let me tell you, we got there way too early, and I knew it meant we had to kill an extra hour. That hour felt like a lifetime sentence. Finally, I walked into the doctor's room and was greeted by a spectacle of circular glasses, all different types. It was like a horror movie. She motioned for me to sit in this chair that looked like it was stolen straight from a bus. Dirty, old, and probably vomited on.

Then, the real fun began. She made me close one eye and told me to read the letters on the screen.

And guess what? I hit a roadblock—I couldn't read past the first line. That's when the doctor hit me with it: I had short-sightedness. My heart just dropped. My mom had been right all along. Why am I even surprised?

There's more! The doc said, "We need to dilate your eyes to figure out your prescription." I had no clue what "dilated" meant, but I didn't expect my mom to suddenly turn into a pro-wrestler, grabbing me and strapping me down in the chair to put drops in my eyes. I mean, I was cool with it, but clearly, my eyes were not. They just kept blinking like crazy. And let's not forget the chorus of people in the waiting room, all telling me that even five-year-olds could handle this like a breeze.

So, after those cursed drops finally made it into my eyes, it felt like someone had poured hot lava into my eyeballs. Ouch! I had to sit like that, eyes closed, for a torturous 30 minutes.

Finally, the moment of truth arrived. I was summoned back to the doctor's lair, and this time, I had to stick my head into this strange contraption. I saw this tiny house with a long, winding pathway leading up to it. For what felt like an eternity, the doc kept tweaking the house's position, and then, she jotted down something on a piece of paper and handed it over to my mom.

Once I got back home, I went down a lot of YouTube videos, trying to figure out what type of glasses would suit me best. I even went all Sherlock Holmes on my own face, determining my face shape. At the end of the day, I called it quits and wondered what tomorrow would bring in this spectacle-filled saga.

DAY 4 – HOW DO I LOOK

Today was a big deal, and I've gotta admit, I was a bit anxious about it. You see, I've never been a fan of how glasses look on people. Some folks pull them off effortlessly and make them a fashion statement, but on me? Nah, it's like they're a burden. Why do I have to pay just to see the world more clearly? And sometimes I can't even notice the difference. It sounds ridiculous, right?

But here's the thing: this wasn't a topic open for discussion. I had to get glasses. So, when the dreaded day arrived, I was understandably nervous. But anyway, I rolled out of bed, got dressed, and made my way to the hospital. As soon as I got there, I was summoned right away. The waiting room staff recognized me, probably from the mini-tantrum I threw yesterday. But when I turned around, my mom was nowhere in sight.

I looked around, and there she was, chatting away with some random old lady. You know, my mom's got this thing where, because we're in her hometown, she knows practically everyone, and she makes it a point to strike up a conversation with each and every one of them.

So, there I stood, awkwardly waiting for her to finish her impromptu social hour. Eventually, she rejoined me, and we finally entered the doctor's room. The doctor glanced at my mom and asked her for the small note she had given her yesterday after my mom's check-up. My mom rummaged through her bag, but the note was nowhere to be found. The doctor gave her the side-eye, and then she turned to me.

"Okay," she said, "you have astigmatism, correct?"

I must've looked as surprised as my mom because she suddenly clarified, "No, she has short-sightedness."

The doctor goes, "Ohhh, they mean the same thing."

Wait, what? I might not be a graduate from the School of Eye Medicine, but I'm pretty sure those two aren't the same thing. She waved it off like it was no biggie and had me sit in the same old chair. This time, she handed me these strange-looking glasses and gestured for me to try them on. The lenses were removable, and she made me read the same letters I'd struggled with before, switching lenses until I finally got it right. It took a while, but I eventually found the perfect match.

And then, my mom returned, triumphant. "I found the paper, and as a matter of fact, it says she's short-sighted."

My mom beamed with pride, and the doctor handed her a new prescription slip. Oh, joy! So, it turns out my prescription was a -0.25, not a massive difference, but it was a big deal to my mom because she believed that as I grew taller, my prescription might change. As for me, well, I knew I'd forever be the short queen I am today.

After that little diagnosis session, we all headed over to an optical shop called "Sams Opticals", which is located opposite Anchal St. John's College, where my mom completed her pre-degree, to get me some glasses. My sister also seemed quite familiar with that place as she studied almost six months at St. John's School almost eight years ago located nearby the college.

Coming back to our business, I must've tried on a gazillion pairs. First, I tried square frames and looked like a total nerd. Then came the round ones, and I resembled Harry Potter in all the wrong ways. Long story short, I tried aviators, framed, cat-eye, oval – you name it, I tried it. None of them felt like "me."

Finally, I tried on some heart-shaped glasses. They were alright, but I still didn't quite feel like myself. Out of all the options, they were the only ones that looked somewhat decent on me. But let's be real, I still looked like a geek.

But hey, I wasn't done yet. It's the 21st century, right? So, why not add some cool features? You know, like glasses that change into sunglasses in the sun or block blue light? I barely wanted to be seen with glasses in the first place, so wearing them outside in the sunlight was out of the question.

They wanted to show me how it worked, as if I didn't get it from the name. But truth be told, it was kinda cool. They brought out a circular glass and a tiny flashlight to show how the blue light disappeared when it passed through the glass. In the end, I opted for the basic option. However, my sister who came with us to assist me ordered one for herself with all the

options in the world. When mom reminded her, she already has two, she warded it off saying that having one more in her treasure is completely fine! Well, that's my sister.

With my prescription handed over, we asked how long it'd take for the glasses to be ready. They said about an hour, so we left them our prescription and headed to the nearest café for some milkshakes. Afterwards, we strolled to a nearby store to pick up some jewelry. That's when I remembered my best friend Aisha's birthday was coming up. So, I grabbed a few earrings for her and decided to hunt for the rest of her gifts elsewhere.

When we returned, my glasses were ready. We picked them up, and my mom was all set to pay with her trusty debit card. But guess what? Her card wasn't cooperating. We grabbed one of my grandpa's old phones to call my dad for help, but for some bizarre reason, the phone refused to turn on. When it finally did, there was no money to make any calls. Awkward!

I don't know if it was the panic in our eyes or what, but the folks at the store probably thought we weren't the stealing type. So, they let us take our glasses home and we promised to come back in the evening for payment or will pay it through Google Pay. By collecting their phone number and account number we left, got back home, and immediately called our dad to show off my new specs. We paid through the second option, as my uncle dismissed the idea of going there once more while he can pay them by Google Pay just by a click through his phone. In Kerala, even the auto drivers and street vendors prefer Google Pay nowadays.

The rest of the day went pretty much like any other day. I barely wore my glasses till date because everyone couldn't resist making fun of me.

DAY 5 – DON'T ABANDON ME

About a year ago, I made a startling discovery: my cousin had a dog. Now, for me, animals have never been my cup of tea. I find them rather annoying, to be honest. It's not that I believe animals lack intelligence, but more that their good intentions can lead to accidents, like an unexpected bite or a scratch that might result in rabies. Given these (mis)conceptions, I've never been ready for the commitment of having a pet. So, when I came to know about my cousin's dog, it's safe to say I was terrified. Encountering a dog by accident would send me sprinting in the opposite direction. That's just me!

My cousin Ambadi shared a similar ideology about animals. But out of curiosity, after learning about pets, he insisted on having a dog. His father, my uncle, without consulting anyone else, got him an Labrador puppy named Rocky, who was just six months old at the time.

Now, who's taking care of Rocky? Well, that responsibility fell on his mom. My aunt became Rocky's owner and caregiver, doing everything for him. In the evenings, she'd let him roam and play freely. It's honestly the funniest thing I've ever witnessed because Ambadi wouldn't go near that dog. Among so-called dog lovers, the dog-human bond is so strong that they even sleep together on the same bed, and in the mornings, you'll find the dog comfortably nestled on their laps.

But Ambadi despises it. So, more often than not, Rocky ends up confined to his cage, which is quite sad to witness. My sister, on the other hand, is determined to get Ambadi to play with the dog. She even went to the extent of threatening him, saying she wouldn't play with him until he touched Rocky.

The most entertaining spectacle occurs when we release Rocky from his cage in the evenings. Seriously, I'm not kidding. Every single time Rocky steps out, Ambadi not only locks the door but also rushes inside the house. He goes a step further by climbing up the stairs, just in case, you know. One time, he even clambered onto a tree when Rocky approached, which I found incredibly amusing.

Recently, we decided to give Rocky a nice bath. Of course, we made Ambadi stand near him while my aunt kept a watchful eye, because, well, we couldn't risk Rocky darting off when he saw the water. We even had to chain him up for added protection. Surprisingly, I got closer to Rocky and even assisted in giving him a bath. But Ambadi? No way! He stood about six feet away, that's how scared he was. It was so funny! Even in a locked cage, he wouldn't dare to look at Rocky.

It seems that Rocky has developed a deep affection for my aunt and has a constant craving for food. Whenever he notices someone nearby, he promptly grabs his plate, almost as if he's asking for a meal. It seems like he's constantly hungry. My aunt later informed me that in the past, they used to provide him with food three or four times daily. However, he has gained excess weight, so the vet advised to limit his meals to just twice a day to prevent potential heart issues due to obesity.

He's the cutest, but that doesn't mean I'm not scared of him. I am, trust me. Nevertheless, I understand why dog lovers adore their four-legged pals. They're incredibly hyperactive and blissfully unaware of your emotions or fatigue; all they want to do is play with you.

However, the dilemma we're in is that we're thinking of giving Rocky away. He yearns for playtime, but no one in our house has the time, and those who do are too petrified of him. It's a rather somber situation. My appuppan particularly despises animals, and as a result, Rocky doesn't receive much love. I genuinely feel bad for him. So, my sister and I made a request to my uncle to find Rocky a new home, preferably with some devoted dog lovers.

DAY 6 – THE BIGGEST LULU IN THE WORLD

I am going to be honest, I didn't find it all that exciting when my sister pitched to my family that we should go to Lulu. Because I have gone to Lulu a thousand times when I was in UAE and it wasn't that special, and I would rather sit at home. Either way, why go to the Biggest LuLu in the World when the biggest mall in the world is only 46 minutes away from where I live? It didn't make sense, but my sister talked about this every day for about a week, and she is great at convincing people.

The main reason why she wanted to go there was because she got her nose pierced a few weeks ago, and she really wanted a new diamond nose ring. If we went to Lulu, we could also buy the nose ring from the Kalyan jewelers there.

So, we headed to Lulu, which is situated in Trivandrum. It was quite a lengthy journey, taking around one and a half hours. Upon our arrival, I noticed a multitude of rickshaws neatly parked along the sides, which intrigued me. Inside these rickshaws were auto drivers, patiently waiting. I couldn't be certain whether they were awaiting passengers to pick up or if they had just dropped someone off and were waiting for them to complete their shopping. If it was the latter, I felt like telling them to hang in there because shopping at a mall like this would likely take at least three hours.

When we entered, I saw some security guards standing at the entrance. I found it really weird, but I carried on my way.

When we reached inside, I realized why my sister wanted us to come here. Unlike the Lulu at UAE, it was like an actual mall and had several stores.

As we exited the parking area, the first thing that caught our attention was Kalyan Jewelers. We decided to step inside, and my sister eagerly began browsing through about 10 different nose rings before settling on one. However, my mom advised her to try it on first to ensure it suited her. Still, she hadn't taken off her initial nose ring since it was first pierced, and she wasn't certain if it had fully healed yet. So, she was convinced she needed to visit the restroom to check, and my aunt joined her.

After waiting for about 10 minutes, my sister returned with her nose ring still in place. It turns out, it hurt too much to remove it, and my aunt was too scared to assist her because of her screams. That's when my mother decided to accompany my sister to the washroom, leaving my aunt with me. It was during this moment that she looked at me and suggested that I would look great with a second ear piercing.

I looked at her and said, "umm do you see how much pain my sister is in, no thank you."

"What if I get a nose piercing like your sister?"

"I frankly don't believe you."

Like, think about it, why would she? She was just saying it to convince me, but then I actually thought about it. I would look good, so I stole my uncle's phone which had mobile data and texted my dada, "Acha should I pierce my ear?"

"Yes, I am out, just do it."

So, with newfound guidance, I decided to just do it now or never. But then I realized, what about my supervisor who is always trying to keep my toe in line for her, every wisp of hair is an issue, but I decided that for official events, I can just take it out.

By that time, my sister came back with her nose bleeding. She was holding a tissue and for some reason looked unfazed. She tried on the nose ring and deemed that it looked spectacular. It was three diamond dots, and it was tiny which was good because we do still go to school so probably no teacher will shout at her.

Then I told my mom my decision to pierce my ears and when I tell you that she grinned. I am telling you that she had all hands-on deck and that settled it. I got a green card from both my parents and 2 other people who are piercing with me. Absolutely nothing can go wrong.

The uncle came out and everything went wrong, my cousin's phone was up and recording as he marked with a pen where he was going to pierce. I saw myself in the mirror one last time and braced myself. He came out again with a miniature version of a gun and a stapler. I gripped my handbag tight as I couldn't see anything. I didn't know what was going on and then suddenly I felt as though my ear just got stapled. It did hurt so much, and my face immediately went into a silent scream position. I looked to my right and saw a group of girls staring at me in pain. They were so amused, and it was written all over their faces. I did not want them to pierce my other ear for several reasons. The main one being that I was in extreme pain, and I don't know if I can go through it again. I braced myself again as he did the other side. I had the same reaction but this time it was ten times worse for reasons I don't know. I was being punched and my desire to know how I looked like rose or like vomit. I went up to the mirror and fell in love with my look. I looked amazing. I never knew that I could even make my ears even though it was bulging red from the pain.

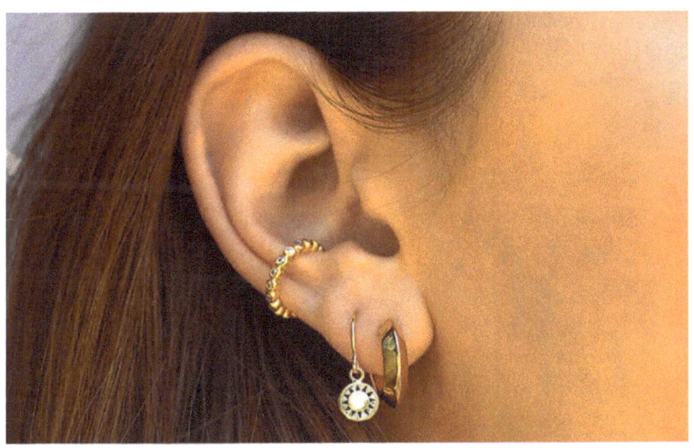

So, it was finally my aunt's turn to step up and keep her promise. The whole family had high hopes for her, especially since two kids half her age had already done it. She couldn't afford to chicken out, but here's the thing: I had to endure the pain twice, while she only had to do it once. Life's unfair, I tell ya. But hey, it was over quicker than I expected, and she looked like she had just been to heaven and back.

Now that we all had something pierced, my cousin felt left out and started screaming about wanting to pierce his ears.

And dye his hair, for crying out loud! But those were impossible requests for my uncle to comprehend, so they were swiftly shut down.

Then we headed to this store my sister was dying to go to, called West Side. Turns out it's some brand from the TATA group. Gotta say, it lived up to all the hype. Their clothes were way better than what we get in Dubai – so modern and stylish. My sister and I ended up grabbing so many clothes that when we finally made it to the dressing room, there was this lady monitoring us, making sure we only took three items inside. It was kinda weird, 'cause I'd never seen a lady in the dressing room before, helping us sort things out. I guess that's just another difference between India and the UAE. But to be fair, I've only traveled to Kerala and Tamil Nadu in India, and even then, I was pretty young.

Inside the dressing room, there were mirrors on all four sides, which reminded me of my mom's old shop. She had the same setup, and it always felt like an optical illusion, with reflections everywhere. It was actually pretty fun, pretending there was a whole crowd of people there.

Every time I tried on clothes, my mom would magically disappear, leaving me awkwardly standing there, waiting for her to come back. In the end, I only bought three out of the four pieces I tried on.

When we went to pay, they gave us a free ChapStick, which has mysteriously vanished now. My cousin was even more furious – not only did he not get his ears pierced, but he also didn't get any new clothes. So, we rushed to another store and got him some Adidas shoes, but he still didn't seem all that satisfied. Then it was my uncle's turn, and we went to get him some clothes too. By this point, we were all pretty exhausted and decided it was prime time to grab some grub.

We hopped on the escalator to reach the food court, and let me tell you, it was packed. We could barely move! We thought about going to "Barbecue Nation" – the place was buzzing, and it's the queen of buffets, just like the Super Bowl is the king of sports. We all agreed on it, except for my uncle, who just wanted a simple dinner. So, that idea was quickly scratched off the list. We settled for the next best option: good ol' McDonald's. Simple, classic, finger-licking food. Or so we thought. I gotta be honest, McDonald's was a major letdown. But hey, at least I managed to eat something. I still can't quite put my finger on what was wrong with it. All I know is that my taste buds were not happy with whatever I had.

Oh, and guess what? I bumped into one of my old friends and his dad there. We exchanged a quick "hi" and "bye," and it was super awkward.

So, after we stuffed our faces, my cousin suddenly had the brilliant idea to go play in the kiddie area. None of us were really interested, but he kept begging and pleading until my mom caved and went with him. Meanwhile, the rest of us decided to hit up a bookstore. I managed to find a murder mystery book, but it didn't quite tickle my fancy. Just as I was about to give up hope, I stumbled upon a decent book. The plot seemed intriguing, and then I noticed some fine print at the top that made me gasp dramatically. Turns out, it was written by none other than Rick Riordan himself! I couldn't believe my eyes. You see, Rick Riordan is my go-to author when I need some comfort reading. I know that anything he writes is bound to be a winner in my book.

Naturally, I snatched it up while my sister went on a book-buying spree and even grabbed a game of Monopoly. Once we were done with our purchases, we went on a mission to find my mom and cousin in Fundora. But for some bizarre reason, *they were nowhere to be found. So, I decided to venture upstairs to the second floor of this amusement park. I walked around for a while, but still no sign of them. Just as I was about to give up, I turned around and bam! My uncle was right there. Apparently, he had come up to help me search when it became clear that they weren't on the lower level. From where I was standing, I could see a bunch of random kids having a blast playing all sorts of games, and I couldn't help but feel a twinge of jealousy. That's when I spotted a rock-climbing wall, something I had always wanted to try. I had only attempted it once before, and let's just say it didn't go too well. Lost in my thoughts, I suddenly noticed my cousin scaling one of the walls like a pro. I immediately called my uncle, and we made our way down to join my sister and aunt, who had already found them.*

My mom was practically bursting with excitement when she saw us. She looked at me and exclaimed, "He's a rock-climbing prodigy! The moment the employees saw him conquer the first wall, they practically begged him to try out the rest. And guess what? He's acing every single level effortlessly. Talk about natural talent!" My mom always got super hyped whenever she saw someone with talent. I couldn't help but feel a tad bit envious, but I had my reasons for not giving it a shot. First off, I was wearing a dress, and secondly, what if I totally sucked at it? I'd never hear the end of it. Plus, I had been feeling pretty queasy lately. So, it was probably best to sit this one out. But still, I couldn't tear my eyes away from my cousin as he conquered each wall with ease. He reached the second-to-last one and returned triumphantly, and we all showered him with congratulations.

But of course, he wasn't done yet. He had his sights set on this ride that looked like a wall of terror, and he refused to go on it alone. And guess who he looked at? Yep, yours truly. I didn't want to be the scaredy-cat who chickened out, and I was pretty sure I could handle it. So, I mustered up some courage, hopped on, and got strapped in. I heard that click, and off we went. Up and down, up and down, and you guessed it, down again. Did I mention earlier that I had been feeling nauseous? Well, that feeling started creeping up on me, but eventually, I got used to it, and by the time it was over, I was feeling somewhat okay.

Finally, we bid farewell to Fabtoora. By that point, we were all pretty tired of wandering around, so we decided to head back home. Gotta say, it was one heck of an exciting day.

DAY 7 – MY NEPHEW

You must be curious about that title in some way. If you're not intrigued, take a moment to reconsider! Well, to put it simply, I have a cousin who never quite felt like a cousin. You know why? Because she is a whopping 18 years older than me. HOW??? Well, my mother's cousin happens to be 13 years older than her, and she had children at a young age too. She had two girls, and the oldest one is Pinky.

Chechi, who is already 30, has two kids. She has always lived close to us, whether it was in India or UAE, so I've always had the pleasure of playing with her kids. In fact, she was even present at my parents' wedding when she was just a child.

Now, let's jump straight into the adventure of the day. Pinky chechi has two sons who are exactly two years apart, almost like a strange family tradition. The older one, Allu, never really took a liking to me. I'm not sure why – I'm pretty awesome, if I do say so myself. My mom thinks I'm overreacting, but seriously, he used to pull my hair and occasionally give me a little hit. Kids, right?

Anyway, there was this one peculiar habit we shared. In order to get his attention, I used to sprint around with my hands behind me, leaning forward. It must have looked quite bizarre, but Allu found it funny and started imitating me. And that's how his signature running style was born. His parents even blamed me for it, although secretly, I'm quite proud of it.

Well, at least it's something I can laugh about when we're older. But this story isn't about Allu; it's about his younger brother, Athu. I hadn't really spent much time with Athu since he was a baby. However, today, I felt a renewed sense of hope. Maybe Athu would adore me, and I could finally outshine my sister.

Our day began with plans to visit Pinky chechi's house. She had gone on an educational trip to Kanyakumari for her BEd course, so obviously Allu needed some way to ensure he wouldn't cry. That's where we came in – the backup plan, or rather, the only plan. Since Pinky chechi knew we were coming, she didn't even send him to daycare in the morning. We had initially planned to go in the morning, but my sister overslept, causing us to delay our visit.

In the evening, we walked to Pinky chechi's house. When Ambadi came back from school, he quickly changed and we all walked together. It wasn't a long walk at all. As we stepped into their house, I must admit, I mistook Athu for Allu at first. They looked so alike, although that perception changed over time.

Next door, there were twins named Lakshmi and Gauri who joined us. One interesting thing about them is that their names were switched when they were young. How am I so sure? Well, it's just a feeling I have. Gauri looks like a Lakshmi, and Lakshmi looks like a Gauri. Perhaps someone made a mistake when they were young and switched their names. It's a bit confusing for my sister and me, but we managed.

We entered the house and joined Athu and Allu. I saw this as the perfect opportunity to bond with Athu, so I invited him to play. To my surprise, he immediately came to me, choosing my company over my sister's. I was overjoyed, walking around *with him in my arms, proudly showing off my newfound favorite person.*

I soon discovered that Lakshmi and Gauri were better at pampering Athu than me. Can you believe it? They actually took a marker and drew moles all over him! I couldn't help but feel a twinge of jealousy. How did the twins manage to capture his attention more than me?

Later on, we all gathered to play a fun game called "Mafia." If you're not familiar with it, it's similar to "police and thief," but with a twist. Instead of cops and robbers, we had villagers and mafia members. The goal was to figure out who was in the mafia. As we played, I realized that in every single round, I never once got to be part of the mafia. It was only when I had given up hope that, miraculously, I finally got to be mafia once! And then, in a strange turn of events, I just couldn't stop being mafia. It's funny how these games work, isn't it?

Soon enough, Lakshmi and Gauri had to finish their notes because they have school tomorrow, unlike us. They bid us farewell and left. It was at that moment that I discovered Allu's and Athu's crazy obsession with biscuits. Even though Athu couldn't eat them, he refused to listen to anyone. That's when I truly bonded with Athu over our shared love for biscuits, even though I didn't particularly enjoy the taste. He would feed me a piece, and then I would break it and give it back to him. It was clear that he loved me more than my sister. He even learned my name, although he said "Mamalu" instead of "Ammalu." But it's practically the same thing, right? So, that solves the big riddle!

As darkness settled in, we realized that the internet had been down since morning, and poor Allu desperately needed his mother's comfort or some Coco Melon videos. Tensions started to rise, and eventually, we decided to call it a day. Since it was getting late and dark, my parents arranged for an auto to pick us up.

When we arrived back home, we found everyone gathered in the hall. The power had been out all day, making cooking impossible. We thought about ordering parotta and chicken from a nearby store, but my grandfather, being old-fashioned, insisted that it would be useless to call them. He couldn't understand who would come to our house late at night. I must admit, I didn't quite understand his logic either. Nevertheless, he decided to step outside for a while, leaving us hungry and puzzled.

We set out on a mission to locate him and discovered the gate wide open, yet our grandfather was nowhere to be found. Concerned passersby on motorcycles stopped to inquire if everything was alright, and we assured them that all was well. Eventually, our grandfather returned, having taken a slight detour. We shared a lighthearted moment, joking about our search for our missing grandfather, although he didn't quite grasp the humor.

With the electricity finally restored, we wrapped up a rather eventful day, pondering how the power outage could have lasted from 8:00 AM to 10:30 PM. Truly, it had been a day filled with unexpected twists.

DAY 8 – AT THE FAMILY TEMPLE

Ugh, today was an early start! I had to drag myself out of bed at 7:30 in the morning. Imagine that! Then it was the whole bath-and-get-dressed routine before I stumbled my way to the car. My cousin brother, my sister, my mom, and my uncle were all piling into the car too. I brought my book along, just in case my sister and I wanted to catch some sleep during the ride. But my mom had other ideas. She said that once we woke up in purpose of going to the temple, we couldn't sleep on the way to the temple.

But here's the cool part. The temple we were going to? Well, it's kind of like our family's place. See, my great-grandfather was the one who built it. How awesome is that?

So, we finally reached a place called Madathara, in Kollam district, located in the foothills of Western Ghats. For me it seems that this temple is deep in the forest. We had to climb down a little hill first, and I kept slipping and sliding all the way. And guess what? We had to walk even more after that! I have observed that the way to the temple is filled with many fruit and timber trees. When I finally spotted the temple, I had to take off my shoes because, from there, we had to walk barefoot. I never knew rocks could be so sharp. Ouch! Eventually, we got to a more paved path. Thank goodness for that!

Immediately I spotted a scruffy-looking guy with dark hair and brown eyes looked about in his thirties maybe. I soon found out he was my mom's cousin brother so my uncle. The thing about being the youngest is that my sister formed many memories when I wasn't born and born but too young to remember. So, my sister knew half the people there. While I knew no one, and all of them thought I was my sister. I felt like a total stranger there.

But you know what I was looking forward to? Making something called 'Ponkala'. It's like a traditional dish, and you make it right there in front of God. Then you get to eat it after the ceremony. The catch was that we had to make it on the ground. We gathered sticks and rocks to create a cooking setup called an adupp (hearth) and got ready to make a fire. I went barefoot all around, trying to find some sticks, but they were all wet because it rained the night before. Just GREAT!

Luckily, one of the aunties from the neighborhood saved the day. She brought some dry wood from her home for us. We weren't allowed to light the fire just yet. So, we sat there and waited for everyone to gather.

That's when I started talking to one of the uncles. First, he chatted with my sister, and then he saw me and started asking if I was "the writer." Seriously? Did they only know me for being an author? Anyway, I said yes, and he got all curious about whether I was working on something for my new book. It's funny how people think writing is so easy, like stories just appear out of thin air.

Finally, it was time to light the Ponkala. We got the fire from the temple, and I carefully carried it to the woodpile. On top of that, we had a pot filled with water. But keeping the fire going was tough; it burned through the wood super-fast. Once the water started boiling, my mom added some rice after saying a prayer. But my eyes were burning from all the smoke. It was unbearable, so my mom told me to go get water from the well.

The well was inside the temple area, and there was a bucket with a little rope thing attached. I dipped it into the well, filled it with water, and tried to pull it up. Man, I must've looked weak because everyone was staring at me, probably judging me too. But somehow, I managed to get it up and handed it over to my mom.

Once the rice was all cooked, my mom added stuff like jaggery, ripe banana pieces, coconut, and cardamom to it. It was called ponkala payasam, and then the priest sprinkled holy water on it during a ritual called nedikkuka.

By this point, my eyes were tearing up from all the smoke, and I just couldn't stand there anymore. So, I kind of wandered off. That's when this auntie in set and mundu with maroon blouse spotted me. By calling my sister's name, she tried to hug me. I didn't want to be rude so I just said I am Ammalu, the younger one and then she turned and saw my sister, who couldn't recognize her at first then she squinted her eyes and said "AMMAMMA"

And then the auntie started crying. My sister was trying her best to calm her down. Later my sister explained that she was the one who had taken care of during her early days, and the way they hugged each other, I can sense that they were pretty close once.

The site where our family temple situated is spectacular. On the left side, we can spot vast rice fields, on the right the rubber plantations and in front of the temple there is a kaav. My mom always feels nostalgic about this place. Almost 35 years back, there was a waterfall over one side of the kaav and my mother during vacation used to take a bath in that waterfall along with her aunties. My grandma told that once there was an excavation in search of graphite (Actually the excavation was conducted in search of gemstone, cat's eye, however, they only got Graphite) and after that eventually it dried up. I made a visit to that area along a wooden bridge which was made from a coconut trunk, still, a small water stream is there.

I wonder how many different types of plants will be there in the kaav. I was informed that every Kerala tharavadu has a kaav back then. (Kaav in Malayalam refers to a sacred groove which has cultural religious significance).

It is a mini ecosystem that typically left undisturbed by human activity. So it serves as a biodiversity hotspot, harboring a wide variety of flora and fauna. These are the places from where traditional medicinal plants are sourced. I consider kaav as a deep-rooted connecting point between man and nature. I am glad to know that my tharavadu has a well-protected Kaav.

Our family owns a rubber estate around here. But here's the sad part, even though my grandma has 7 siblings, none of them live there anymore. The land, around 40 acres with rubber trees, just sits there. I even saw the remains of our old family home, which got partially wrecked during road construction.

I inquired about the history of our temple too. It is called Koorappally temple. My great-great-grandfather (Kilimanoor Keezhperoor Madavan Pillai) came to Kottarakkara concert for a lawsuit, and learned that there was some agricultural land for sale in a place called Madathara in the east. He along with his friends came here by walking and I wondered how many days he might have taken to reach there! I guess there was a small temple belonged to 'adivasis' (tribal communities) there and later it was converted to this form in 1956 by my great-grandfather, Koorappally R. Ramakrishna Pillai. I was also informed that the meaning of Koorappalli is 'old school'.

I helped to light the fire in a gigantic intricately designed 'kal vilakku' (oil lamp) which is situated in front of the temple. I was informed that lighting kalvilakku will purify the temple premises along with the spiritual illumination of devotees' mind and soul.

After ponkala, we attended 'deeparadhana' and did the Archana pooja. Afterwards, we all sat down on the floor with legs crossed and ate kanji ("rice porridge" or "rice gruel." Kanji is a popular South Indian and Kerala dish made from boiled rice and water) and payar (green gram) which was prepared at the temple premises. Instead of spoons, plavila karandis made of green jack leaves were given. I was seeing those for the first time in my life. And we three ate together from a plate and I would say it was so delicious and yummy.

There was a banana next to me, so I asked my Kiran Uncle if he wanted one in English, and he didn't seem to understand it. So, I decided to show my Malayalam speaking skills and enquired "ninakku veno?" (Do you want?)

My entire family turned to me in shock. What did you just say? What I didn't know was that it was informal language, and we should not use "ninakku" to elders. Those uncles could not let it go and what was worse was that we were going to visit their home in their car. So, during the entire ride, they were making fun of me. I honestly got so mad but I didn't want to show it, so I pretended to sleep.

On our way back home, we visited two of our relatives' houses and we shared our ponkala payasam with them. 'And I harvested red guava and cherries directly from trees using a local tool known as a "thotta" stick. It was indeed a delightful and adventurous experience for me.

Since I have seen and experienced the beauty of nature in Madathara, I learned more about this area and found out the tourist places located nearby. For those in Thiruvananthapuram or Kollam seeking the Ooty ambiance, consider a visit to Thenmala eco-tourism. It offers activities like rock climbing, river crossing, and butterfly watching at Thenmala Butterfly Safari Park.

Arippa is another dream destination, which is an extension of Thenmala eco-tourism project, a 10-minute drive from Madathara. Hills, valleys, plains, streams, cascades, towering trees, medicinal plants, birds, and animals – the woods at

Arippa thrum with life, and after a time you walk ecstatically, abandoning yourself totally in the sheer bliss of being there as a pilgrim to Mother Earth. The virgin land of Arippa is located on the edge of Thiruvananthapuram-Shenkottai State Highway. Besides this, the visitors can learn about the traditions and way of life of the tribal communities. Arippa is 2 hours travel from Thiruvananthapuram. I assure you it is worth the time. I have visited Thenmala before the era of pandemic and aspire to visit Arippa next time with my father.

On the way back to Kottukkal, we encountered something special. Two Green Army members (Haritha Karma Sena) in greenish-blue uniforms collected plastics from my grandmother. I have learned that this initiative, supported by local bodies, focuses on recycling non-biodegradable waste. They visit houses monthly, charging a nominal fee of Rs. 50 for collecting washed and dried plastic bags. This not only benefits the environment but also empowers marginalized women.

As a student studying democracy and local governance, witnessing the Green Army in action was inspiring. We also shared our payasam with them, and their warm acceptance brought joy to the day. This experience showcases the positive impact of local bodies on both the environment and society.

I have to mention our neighborhood's streetlights too at this point. You see, it is up to us, the locals, to take care of them. So, every evening, my grandpa (we call him "appooppan") or my cousin Ambadi and I would head over to the streetlights near our house to switch them on at night and make sure they were turned off during the day. I felt like a responsible citizen.

DAY 9 – HANGING OFF A CLIFF

Today was the day we'd all been eagerly waiting for. Well, I had been anticipating it ever since my dad returned from India back in March. One of the first things he raved about was going to the Varkala beach at night. He made it sound absolutely spectacular, so there was no way my family and I were going to miss out on this adventure.

By hearing this, you may think that Varkala is a far-away place. Nope! It is where my father's ancestral home is situated. Even though we have visited Varkala cliff numerous times during daytime but never at night hours. Before going there, I did a thorough research on the specialties of that place. Let me share those with you.

Varkala is a coastal town in the southern state of Kerala, well known as a tourist place, the main attractions are Varkala cliff and beach. Varkala cliff is a unique geographical formation that runs along the Arabian Sea Coast. It is a picturesque stretch of red laterite cliffs, rising dramatically from shoreline. It offers mesmerizing panoramic views of the Arabian Sea, making it a popular spot for locals and many tourists from India and abroad. You can see lots of shops, cafes and restaurants, tattoo centers, etc. Moreover, Varkala is a hub of Ayurvedic resorts and Yoga centers.

Varkala beach is also known as Papanasam beach. Locals believe that the natural spring here is magical with medicinal and spiritual properties and if you take a dip here, it will wash away all your sins. Sounds cool.

A 2000-year-old Hindu temple is also located nearby the beach, dedicated to Lord Vishnu.

If you wish to make a visit to Varkala cliff, never miss out on a coastal village located near it, called Kappil. I would say Kappil beach is an extension of Varkala beach but offers a quieter atmosphere. It is where Kappil lake converges with the Arabian Sea, which creates a stunning landscape and lush greenery. It also offers boating services. I was informed that my parents' post-wedding photo shoots were done in Kappil.

As we got dressed and piled into the car, a sense of excitement began to creep over me. Our first stop was at one of our relatives' houses to pick up the key to my dad's house. To be honest, I was a bit hesitant about going to that house. It had practically been abandoned for months, and that gave me the creeps. But I pushed those thoughts aside and followed my family into our relative's house.

They tried to make me eat a giant banana. You know, one of those really long ones that no one likes. So, I nibbled a bit and handed the rest to my mom with a polite smile. Dodged that banana bullet!

Since we were already at the relative's place, my mom, sister, and I decided to pay a visit to my dad's cousins who lived nearby. But when we stepped outside, I noticed my shoes. It would have taken me ages to put them on, and sheer laziness got the best of me. I swiped my mom's shoes instead. She got pretty mad and didn't even spare me a glance as she asked my other uncle (seriously, I have too many uncles) for a pair of shoes. He gave me the ones he was wearing and went on walking barefoot. I felt so guilty, and I immediately protested, but he assured me it was fine. I still felt bad, though.

After securing the key and saying our goodbyes, we finally set off for the beach. The first thing that caught my eye was a bunch of guys selling LED lights in bottles and necklaces you could hang around your neck. Cool, right? As we strolled further, the beach came into view. But there was a downer – we couldn't go down to the beach as it was nighttime.

However, as we wandered on, we found rows and rows of restaurants and shops. Some shops had these cute hand-knit bags that I liked, but they were too heavy for my taste. Then there were the restaurants, DJ-style, blasting the most famous TikTok songs. Ultimately, we settled on one restaurant with a perfect view of the beach. I soon realized there were no fans anywhere, but I still felt chilly. Everyone knows the beach is not a fan of warmth.

The one thing I'd been craving since I arrived was pasta. Back home, whenever I wanted something spicy, I'd just whip up a pot of pasta and make my own sauce. But in India, I was devastated to find out that pasta bundles weren't waiting for me. So, when we ordered, I went for white sauce seafood pasta. My mom ordered noodles, and my cousin practically wanted to order everything on the menu. When my pasta arrived, I couldn't have been happier. My taste buds went wild with the flavor of pasta. It felt like forever since I'd last tasted it.

After our delicious meal, we headed back to my dad's house. As soon as I stepped inside, a sudden chill ran down my spine. The only reason I used to enjoy coming here before was because there were always people to play with. But now, there was no one. The house somehow still smelled the same and looked as clean as ever. We went upstairs to choose beds to sleep in, but all the rooms were really hot because the windows were always closed, so no cool air could come in. Plus, all the ACs weren't working. My uncle and auntie managed to find a room with a working fan and decided to sleep there. The rest of us, my mom, my sister, my cousin, and I, grabbed mattresses from other rooms and created a makeshift bed.

I tried to read a book and get some sleep, but no matter how hard I tried, it was impossible. I wasn't sure if it was because it was so hot or because the floor was uncomfortably hard. Either way, I ended up falling asleep around 3 am, and I felt absolutely terrible.

DAY 10 – THE FIVE PIERCINGS

I woke up way too early, like at the ungodly hour of 7 am. You know that feeling when you haven't had enough sleep? Yeah, that was me. Dragging myself out of bed, I changed into some random clothes. Our first order of business was to return the keys to the relative. But guess what? They tried to force-feed me a banana again, and as usual, I refused politely.

Next, we were headed to my cousin's place, which I was pretty excited about. In the UAE, they live just a stone's throw away, like literally a two-minute drive. So, you could say we're pretty close.

However, on the way there, we got lost, like super lost. We had to call them for directions, and when we finally arrived, I walked into the house to find some random dude sitting with my cousins. Apparently, he was another cousin, but from their mom's side, so no blood relation to me. I immediately ran to my baby cousin and gave him a bear hug. Then, I had some appam and chicken curry, which was delicious, and raced upstairs to play Monopoly, our family game.

We played for a mere 5 minutes, and just when I was on the verge of winning (which almost never happens, mind you, because I have the worst luck), my mom called us downstairs. So close, yet so far from victory. Anyway, I knew that when we got back home, I'd be stuck with nothing to do, so I really wanted to stay and see how the game ended. Especially since my cousin, Amal, had spent all his money building houses on the cheapest property that no one ever lands on. I was curious to see what would happen.

When we descended, my kochachan (My father's brother) thought it was the perfect time to capture the moment with a photo. We took like nine photos, I kid you not. It was then that I spotted two dogs in a cage. Now, let me clarify something about these dogs. They look super tiny, so you'd think they're like 2 months old, but in reality, they're like 6 years old. They go by the names Timon and Simba, like the characters from "The Lion King," and they're super energetic.

Now, I've got to tell you, I'm a total scaredy-cat. I'm scared of a bunch of things, and one of them is dogs in cages. They look cute up close, but they terrify me, so my usual reaction is to run. But that tactic doesn't always work out. In fact, it usually backfires because they think I want to play, and they start chasing me.

After our goodbyes, we hopped into the car and headed to the jewelry store. You see, my aunt had recently pierced her nose, but she hadn't switched out the initial stud for a regular nose ring yet. Those piercing guns usually come with a small gold ball nose ring, which tends to lose its color over time. It's essential to replace it after about a week to avoid any potential infections. And I needed to change mine too, so it was a win-win situation, I guess.

When we got there, we were greeted by a lady in a sari. After explaining that we wanted to buy a nose ring and a second stud earring, she directed us to the elevator, and we headed to the second floor. There, we were seated at a clear glass table with all the nose rings on display. The games began. My aunt tried on at least eight of them, and I thought they all looked gorgeous. But my mom and sister had a problem with each and every one. Then she tried on a diamond-studded star nose ring, and I thought they'd immediately reject it. Surprisingly, they didn't hate it, so they put it aside and started going through more options. Eventually, they decided the star was the best one, but since it was going to be expensive, my aunt decided to try it on first. We were all pretty sure this wouldn't end well.

Since the initial stud was in my ear, you could see the back of it. Unlike my aunt's, mine was visible. So, I became the guinea pig, and they all started fiddling with the back of my earring. They turned it, twisted it, and even tried to pull it apart, but nothing seemed to work. Then, a nearby worker probably saw our struggle and informed us that there was a guy on the first floor who could remove the initial stud for us. So, we went downstairs hand in hand.

Now, I'm pretty sure that at some point, everyone has wanted to go inside those rooms that are marked "staff only, do not enter." Well, I'm no exception, and today, I got my chance. It was a small square room, and there was a man sitting on the floor with his legs crossed, melting gold with a lighter and attaching a needle to the back of a nose ring using fire. When the lady knocked on the already open door, he looked up, and she explained the situation to him. He immediately got up and told my aunt to sit in the chair. It was as if it was no big deal. He simply dug his finger inside her nose and removed the back of the nosering. Apparently, all you had to do was pull it off. Then it was my turn.

Now, remember how I mentioned I'm a huge scaredy-cat and that I'm scared of anything that causes me pain? Well, I started wriggling in the chair and begged for just one more minute with it. My initial stud was still intact, and I wasn't ready to let go. Eventually, everyone got tired of my antics, and a worker auntie held my hands as they took off the earring. I felt the same sharp pain that I did when I first got the piercing – it starts off painful, then numbs for a while, and then suddenly hits you like a wrecking ball. Complicated, right? I know.

After that ordeal, my aunt and I headed back upstairs. She immediately tried on the star nose ring again, and, unexpectedly, everyone liked it.

So, we moved to a different section where they had second stud earrings. I sifted through a bunch of them, but I didn't like any of them. Eventually, I told them I wanted a hoop earring because I used to have one, but it broke. The lady behind the counter lit up and brought out a box filled with different hoop earrings. I eventually chose a gold one with diamonds on the rim, and surprisingly, it looked really good when I tried it on. So, I decided on that one, and they allowed me to leave it on since they had seen how much pain I was in earlier.

We made our way downstairs to pay for everything. However, we ran into a problem – when my aunt tried on the nosering, she didn't try on the back part, and now it seemed impossible to put it on. The other side just disappeared, it seemed. So, we went to the man in the room, and he informed us that her nose was swollen. He suggested applying some medicine, and after a few days, she'd be able to wear it. I decided to remove my initial stud as well. I approached my uncle because, like I mentioned earlier, I was pretty scared of that chair. My uncle simply popped it open, and when I turned to put in my other hoop earring, I saw my mom in the chair. Apparently, she was going to pierce her nose again. Yup, she'd done it before, but it closed up because her nose was too big. Now, she was doing it all over again. Initially, I was excited because my mom always complains about how much I overreact, and this would be perfect payback. But then I realized that now all three of them had nose piercings, and I was the only one left out. But it was fine.

Turns out, when my aunt was choosing nose rings, she came across one and took it, saying she'd pierce her nose later. But due to peer pressure, she decided to do it right then and there. She clutched her bag for dear life as they slipped a needle through her nose, which was connected to the nose ring. As they removed the needle part and added the push-back, she still stood there all tense. After we reminded her to relax, I finally got a good look at her new nose ring, and I have to say it suited her perfectly.

With everything paid for, we left and headed to a nearby restaurant. We ordered pasta, because ever since I got everyone in the mood for pasta when we went to the beach, all they wanted was pasta. Unfortunately, when the food arrived, it turned out to be pasta with red sauce instead of white sauce. I was hesitant, but it still tasted good. After that, we headed back home, and I spent the rest of the day catching up on episodes of shows airing during the weekends before eventually dozing off.

DAY 11 – THE HAIR DISASTER

So, like I was saying earlier, the hair-coloring madness struck our family. My sister had already transformed her hair into something wild, and now my mom and aunt decided it was their turn to join the party. Off we went to "Kavi's Salon," a place just a hop, skip, and a jump away from our home, about a 5-minute drive. As we arrived, the aunties were there to greet us with playful banter, joking about how we should have brought electricity along since they were experiencing a power outage.

It turned out that the salon had lost electricity, and their backup power was ruined too. So, coloring hair in the dark was a no-go. We had to retreat and have lunch at home while waiting for the power to come back on.

Returning in my uncle's car, I noticed a jar of candy in the backseat. With my uncle's blessing, I decided to take it to the salon for the ladies there because, well, I'm such a sweet person.

Sadly, when we returned, the electricity was still playing hide and seek. But since there were no other customers around, the lady at the salon decided to start cutting their hair because, luckily, that didn't require electricity.

With my mom and aunt off to get their hair washed, I was left twiddling my thumbs. So, I decided to spread some cheer and handed out chocolates to everyone. That's when people finally started taking an interest in me.

What I don't get is why these aunties pretend to be on diets. I mean, if you want the chocolate, just take it! No need for the whole "I couldn't" and "I'm on a diet" charade. And the worst are those who pretend they don't like chocolate. Seriously, who doesn't like chocolate?

When it came time for my mom to make a decision about her hair, we ran into a little dilemma. You see, my mom and I both suffer from severe commitment and trust issues. So, we did the most logical thing and called my sister, who has no such hang-ups. She gave the green light, and my mom was still on the fence until the stylist promised it would be just a minor trim.

While they were getting their hair done, they had to sit there awkwardly because, without electricity, blow-drying wasn't an option. They engaged in small talk to pass the time, so I did the smart thing and explored the other rooms in the salon.

I wandered into a room with a huge bed and a cart filled with various products like serums, toners, bleach, and stuff. I didn't recognize most of them, but I assumed they were probably high-end brands. You know those TikToks where pretty people pile on a bunch of stuff and claim it's their secret to great skin? Yeah, it reminded me of that. Although secretly, I wanted to open everything just for the fun of it.

But before I could start digging into the products, a sudden cold breeze hit me. The electricity was back! I watched as the staff rushed to grab the blow dryers. They managed to dry hair for about 5 minutes, but then, in classic fashion, the electricity decided to play the on-and-off game. It was beyond frustrating for everyone.

After much back-and-forth, the power finally stayed on. I have to admit, my mom's hair looked the same but different. It's hard to explain, but it was intriguing. Suddenly, my sister let out a joyful scream. I wasn't too surprised because my sister tends to react that way to most things. But when I turned around, I saw my cousin. I know what you're thinking, "Is this cousin number 8?" Well, I'm not entirely sure, but you might recall her. Behold, it was none other than Pinky Chechi, the cousin who's 18 years older than me.

Apparently, she came to the salon for threading, and when she saw so many shoes outside, she thought she'd have to return later. But as she was about to leave, she spotted my sister through the window and decided to come in.

After getting threaded, Pinky Chechi kindly invited me to her house to play with the kids because she thought I might be bored. So, we hopped on her scooty, which is the preferred mode of transportation for ladies in the neighborhood.

When we arrived, I met Athu, Pinky Chechi's younger son, who was quite fond of me. However, Allu, the older one, not so much. As soon as I saw Athu, he came from behind, playfully poking and lifting my frock, asking where my butt was. It was quite the enchanting experience.

I spent the entire day trying to entertain Athu. One thing I quickly discovered was his love for people jumping. Why, you ask? Well, nobody knows, but if you start jumping, he won't let you stop, shouting "CHADDU!" which means "jump" in Malayalam. This little one was truly testing my athletic abilities. I was gasping for air until I could find something else to distract him with.

As time passed, curiosity got the best of me, and I wanted to know what happened to my mom and aunt's hair. I told chechi about it and walked back to the salon. Inside, my aunt was still in the chair, my sister was sitting next to her, but my mom was nowhere in sight. My sister had a big grin on her face, obviously eager to share some news.

"Guess what!" she exclaimed. I leaned in closer, and she continued, "Amma's hair can't be dyed." Apparently, my mom had dyed her hair black so many times that the new color wouldn't

stick. So, she essentially spent all that money on products for nothing.

I asked where my mom was, and my sister pointed to another room. Since her hair couldn't be colored, she decided to at least get a facial. I mean, think about it – she had spent nearly 8 hours there, and she came home looking exactly the same. I couldn't help but wonder if she was secretly sad about it. So, I asked her if she was, but she calmly replied, "Nope, I didn't really want to commit to this either way, and I didn't feel like it would suit my face. So, this is a relief."

A little while later, my aunt decided she wanted a facial too. It was already 9 pm, and I was itching to go home. Now I had to wait for their facials to finish.

When I was younger, I always thought facials would make people look better. But seeing my mom and aunt after their facials, I couldn't see much of a difference. So, I wondered if the salon had pulled a fast one on us.

Finally, my uncle arrived after what felt like an eternity. My sister and I immediately hopped into the car and waited for my mom. After she paid and hopped in, we headed home, which took barely 5 minutes. When we got there, my grandma immediately reached for her glasses to get a good look at her daughter and daughter-in-law's new hair. But she was in for a surprise when she barely noticed any change. She didn't seem to react much and just left.

And with that, our day of hair-coloring escapades came to an end.

DAY 12 – DYING IN THE CAR

I've got a secret – I absolutely despise long trips, but this time, I had no choice! We'd been planning this journey to Guruvayur for ages, but it kept getting delayed. First, my period decided to throw a curveball and stuck around longer than expected. After a week of waiting, we said, "Let's just go!" I'd stay at my aunt's place while the others went to the temple.

Little did I know, this trip would turn into a never-ending 10-hour marathon! Seriously, it was a serious test of patience, especially for someone like me who gets car sick. But hey, I thought, "What the heck, let's do it!" I tend to be a bit overly optimistic sometimes.

So, we made a special request to sit in the backseat, and my cousin made a fuss about it. But eventually, everyone settled into their spots. I, however, was living the dream in the back with all the suitcases. You see, I've always had a soft spot for the backseat. Most people prefer the front for legroom and conversation, but not me. I'd take two seats in the back any day. Plus, if my seatmate was feeling generous, I could even catch some nap on their lap. It's like a luxury suite back there!

The backseat had always been my safe haven, and I had some pretty good reasons for it. More space, especially when it's just my mom, sister, dad, and me on these trips. And, of course, those two seats and the nap option – who could resist? Front seat folks are missing out; I'd rather be snoozing.

But this time, there was a twist. I hopped into the car and realized there was only one seat available in the back because the other two were piled high with suitcases. So, I squeezed in and made it work. Luckily, I have a superpower – I can sleep anywhere. I moved a suitcase close, used the zipper as a pillow, and curled up on the seat. It was surprisingly comfy, and I drifted off in no time.

And then... BANG! I was jolted awake by a massive thud next to my ear. The suitcase fell on top of me, and I started yelling, "AMMA AMMMMMAAAAAAA" (which means "mom" in Malayalam). But, there was no response. It was my sister who eventually turned around and rescued me from beneath the suitcase. After that mini-drama, my mom turned around and said, "Ente Kunju" (which means "my baby") in a sympathetic voice. I couldn't help but yell, "WHY DIDN'T YOU HELP ME WHEN I WAS SCREAMING?" Her reply? "Actually, I thought it was your cousin crying for something again." Talk about a misunderstanding.

Time passed, and our stomachs started growling for snacks. We made a pitstop next to some random Indian tea shops. While my aunt and cousin ventured out to grab snacks, they woke me up. You won't believe the snack haul they brought back! It was like a treasure trove, all packed into a small green bag. First, there was a long chain of chips, all stuck together at the back, like a cream onion flavor. My sister tore the back of the chips, and suddenly, I was ravenous. I don't even remember what happened next. I just inhaled snacks, chocolate chips, and even a bit of cake. Note to self: never get in a car after a snack binge. I felt nauseous, and it was not pleasant.

But, as usual, I tried to go back to sleep. I lay on the same suitcase that fell on my head earlier, but it was rough. So, I switched to the one below it, made of fabric, and it felt so much better.

After a while, everyone got hungry again, and we stopped at a proper shop near Alappuzha-Ernakulam highway. Everyone got out except my sister and me. They bought banana-coated-with-crust (Pazhampori) and this strange vada that didn't taste like a vada at all. It was sweet, fluffy, and spicy because it had tiny chili bits in it. I'm not kidding; it was the best vada I've ever had in my life. Sadly, it disappeared faster than I could blink. The crowd near that shop must know their snacks.

And then, I realized I'd written like four paragraphs just describing food. Oops, typical me. Anyway, I was basically dying of boredom in that car. It had been, like, six hours of sitting around with nothing to do. No phone, no book, just me, my family, and my thoughts. I was so bored it was driving me insane. My only entertainment was watching my sister try to navigate my uncle's driving blunders. Clever, right?

When we reached Lulu at Ernakulam, my sister suddenly had the urge to visit. So, we decided to make a quick stop, and that's when things got interesting. You see, people were giving us weird looks. Why? Because my mom and aunt were dressed in saris. Apparently, no one dresses up that fancy for a mall. It's a long story, but we were originally planning to visit a temple on the way to Thrissur, but things didn't go as planned, so we were left with our fancy attire.

We ended up at West Side and bought some clothes. My uncle called to hurry us up, so we rushed through our shopping. But on our way back, we spotted some doughnuts, and my eyes landed on a chewy-looking cookie. My mom was all like, "Nah," but when I asked for a cookie, the shopkeeper gave me a sample. Thank goodness my mom told me not to buy it because it tasted terrible. And then, we rushed back to the car.

Now, it was nighttime, about three hours later, and my butt hurt from sitting so long. I couldn't even tell if I was going insane or not. Plus, it was almost midnight. So, we decided to grab a bite at a restaurant, but we couldn't agree on which one to go to. First, we were all about Saravana Bhavan, but we missed the exit. Then, we passed by four different restaurants, but every time, we found excuses not to go in. We drove so far that we started worrying there wouldn't be any restaurants left. Finally, we spotted an open restaurant with tables outside, and it looked promising.

We parked and went inside. When I stepped out of the car, my legs felt like they'd never walked before. I started doing a bunch of stretches because sitting for so long had taken a toll on my body. And guess what? Everyone else felt the same way. After settling in, we realized we weren't all that hungry because we'd eaten a ton of snacks. So, my sister and I ordered cheesy fries, my mom and aunt shared a small plate of noodles, and my uncle ordered a masala dosa. But my cousin, well, he's always hungry, so he went all-in with a Beastie burger. When it arrived, it was, like, so he ordered the Beastie burger and when I came I kid you not it was so big, it was twice the size of his mouth. He literally divided it in half and squished it down flat so that he could fit it into his mouth but apparently it tasted amazing after he finished the first half, he was sure that he had no room left for another half. So, we went to grab the other half when we could all finish it together but my cousin grabbed it right out of our hands.

And he soon finished that too and the cheesy fries and they were pretty good. Then we made our way to the car again and this time I convinced my cousin to go sit in the back because I'm pretty sure if I sit in the back, squished with all those suitcases again I was gonna die!

Now we were only 20 minutes away from our destination and honestly that was such a relief cause I couldn't wait to sleep and since it was pretty much 11:30 at that point and really close to 12. While we were going there we got stopped by the police because it was the police's job to make sure that there *was no suspicious activity going around because it's literally midnight which I actually found pretty surprising because in UAE even if it was 2:00 AM no one would bat an eye.*

When we finally reached the neighborhood in which her house is located, we got so confused because it was just a narrow road with many curves and turns and all the buildings were exactly the same. So, we hit her up not expecting her to pick up as it was so late but surprisingly she did but we couldn't figure out where we were. So my big brain just shouted a nearby sign I don't really remember what it was right now but right after she heard that she gave us some directions and we finally reached.

We opened the gate and parked the car in front of the building when we got out she and her daughter were standing there. I have got to admit the flat looked pretty cool. We then climbed the stairs because there was no lift and I was actually pretty bummed out cause I don't do well with stairs. Stairs are basically my enemy, whenever I climb them, I feel like passing out each time and they always take my breath away and not in a good way but her flat was on the first floor so it wasn't that bad.

When we got in we got greeted by a Hall with no couch which wasn't that bad. We immediately changed and went to sleep. I actually found it pretty weird that they had two rooms cause only her and her small daughter lived there and then we inquired about it she told us it was because one of them was a guestroom cause her husband who is pretty far away comes there sometimes or her mother-in-law make visits.

I slept on the bed along with my other aunt and her daughter. On the floor my sister and my mom slept. And I didn't even realize but I fell asleep in the first 20 minutes which is actually a record for me.

DAY 13 – I AM ABANDONED

I had to wake up bright and early in the morning, the good old time of 4:00 AM. I am not kidding when I tell you that it was too early for me to function. Either way, I grudgingly woke up and everyone was slowly getting dressed because pretty much everyone did not want to get up and leave. But eventually, after like 30 minutes, everyone got dressed. And even my younger cousin Kamalu wanted to join, and she had her very own closet filled with makeup to put on. It was honestly the cutest thing I've ever seen, and she knew exactly what to put on. She was even putting makeup on my aunt, but when I asked her if she would put makeup on me, she said no and that I didn't need any. It was pretty much a backhanded compliment, but like thank you Kamalu. And my mom was particularly jealous when she saw my aunt wearing a pavada, which she wore maybe in eighth grade because it still fits her, and honestly, I was shocked too.

Eventually, after everyone got dressed, we started to head out to the car. The ride wasn't that long, maybe 20 minutes passed by when we reached the temple. I can't even explain to you how huge it was, and by the entrance, there were a bunch of shops filled with miniature gods and bracelets and toys. But we ignored all that and made our way to the temple. Apparently, no cameras or basically any belongings were allowed inside, so everyone gave all their belongings to me to hold outside. They made me sit on this ledge next to the wall where a bunch of people were sitting. I sat down next to an old lady.

Then my entire family bid me farewell, and then I saw the line to get into the temple. It was so long that I am pretty sure it extended back to UAE. So obviously, it would take a long time for them to come out, so it's pretty much just sitting there to waste time.

After some time of sitting there, I saw this tiny little baby walk up towards me. Well, technically she wasn't coming up towards me but was coming up to her mother, but she was sitting right beside me, so technically I had complete authority to play with her. My little cousin Kamalu had one of these weird funky glasses that she gave me to protect. So what better thing to do with them than give it to the baby? I put it on the baby, and she was immediately attached to it. She started to show it off to all of the people beside her and just waiting for them to praise her, and it was honestly so funny that I reached in and took my uncle's phone and took a picture.

But then I realized that she can't keep it because my little cousin Kamalu will probably kill me if her favorite (and only) pair of sunglasses is given away. I tried to get it back, but the little baby was too attached. She was not in the mood to give it to anyone, so her mom decided to play tricks with her.

She said, "Oh, the chechi will cry if you don't give it back."

It took me a minute to realize I was the chechi (frankly because I have never been called chechi), so I did the obvious. What better thing to do than to play along? So I pretended I was crying. It wasn't the most Oscar-worthy performance, but it did the job. She gave it back, well not willingly of course. She was rolling her eyes the whole time (like hello baby, where did you get all this sass from?).

After some time, they both left, leaving me all alone again. I was just thinking about how I had to sit there for so long until they had to come back. I opened the phone and started going *through some pictures of my uncle, but there was literally nothing interesting, so I put the phone back into my mom's purse and just stared around to see if there was anything interesting. Eventually, the grandma sitting next to me decided to ask me a question.*

She asked, "what day is it today?" (in Malayalam)

I obviously had to reply in Malayalam, and mind you; even though I have learned Malayalam my entire life for straight seven years, that doesn't mean I know the days of the week. Then she asked Saturday or Sunday in Malayalam, and I didn't know either. I don't want to tell her I don't know Malayalam because that would be just embarrassing, as she'll be like, "Oh my gosh, this generation."

So, I decided to just take a leap of faith and say the first one. She just nodded and then eventually got up and left.

Then when I turned to my left, I saw my family walking towards me. I was pretty sure there was something on the other side of the temple. I started giving them looks; they definitely saw me and then they're like, "Come, let's go."

I got so surprised because I'm pretty sure it's not been more than like 30 minutes. How did they already come back? Did they pay for some fast pass or something? I just couldn't process it, but then I just got up and started walking, and eventually, I found out that the line was so long that it stretched up to the road, and they weren't willing to wait that long, so they just went inside the temple, gave some offerings, and then left. Certainly, the cards were dealt in my favor.

Then we left the temple and went to go eat breakfast because it was really early in the morning when we reached. I ordered a masala dosa (again, it's pronounced dosha, not dosa), and my uncle also ordered a masala dosa, and so did my sister. But my two younger cousins each bought dosa and paneer, which I didn't know was an option, and I honestly would have ordered that, but now I can't anymore, so it's fine. When the food came, I ate up the masala dosa, and there was a lot of paneer left, so I took a nearby vada, and I just ate paneer with the vada. When I first dipped it in, my cousin gave me the nastiest look, as if I dared to put that into my mouth and steal his paneer, but I did it anyway, so it's all fine.

Then we just left and went back into the temple to look at all the shops. My sister and cousin both got God keychains, and my sister bought the Shiva one because her name is Shiva, and my cousin bought literally every single keychain. There is this thing about him that if he sees something, he wants it, even if he doesn't know what it is, and most of the time, it's the ugliest things ever, and everyone tells him not to buy it, but then he still buys it.

And while he was pleading with literally everyone to buy him the toys, I saw this Spiderman on a stand rotating, and in the middle was a magnet. I was trying to make the Spiderman stand still, but then every time I brought it close to the magnet, it would just fling away. My big science brain knew exactly what was going on – there was a magnet under the Spiderman, so that's why it kept moving. How do I know this? Because before, we used to have this chess set which had magnets on the bottom of the chess pieces so that they would stick to the board. I would always take all the chess pieces and put them underneath each other to try and make them stick. Sometimes they wouldn't stick and would flick away, while other times they would. So, when we learned about the north and south poles of magnets in school, it just stuck in my mind. I knew immediately what it was, and I started telling literally everyone to show how smart I am. Honestly, looking back, no one cared, but to me, it is a new scientific breakthrough, OK?

And then we went into this other shop. My mom always wanted a Krishna statue to put in front of our house, but she never got one. When we went to the store, we found one, and my mom immediately bought it because she said that it looks like my sister, so I guess that's a good thing. While my mom was buying it, the sales associate there was looking at all the Krishna statues and said, "Some people think that if you have a statue that has Krishna blowing his flute, it symbolizes that he's blowing all your happiness away, so you shouldn't get them."

My mom immediately looked up at her, but the sales associate just shrugged and continued, "But honestly, who would

believe in that stuff? Because the flute was the most favorite thing of Krishna, so why would it ever bring you something bad like being sad and unhappy all the time? It makes no sense, right?"

My mom felt like she won the lottery right then and there because she chose the Krishna which wasn't blowing a flute, but one that had it in his arm. Later, I felt pretty sad because I didn't have my own Krishna to put anywhere, and that's when I spotted a miniature blue Krishna sitting in the midst of kunnikkuru, with a peacock feather behind, eating something (later I have learned that it is venna/butter, the favorite cuisine of Krishna) from a jug. I'm like, wow! That is so miniature and would fit perfectly on my table. So, I got it, and now it is trapped on my table. Honestly, I feel like it brings some luck to me now as I feel so productive suddenly, so I'm pretty sure it works.

After we left from there, we went to a convenience store for absolute funzies and bought so much ice cream. But I was pretty full because not only did I eat an entire masala dosa which was the length of the entire plate, but I also had a bunch of vada with paneer, so I am pretty full. What I had was like this mango popsicle, and my mom had an ice cream. She said that she wanted a mango popsicle, so I gave that to her. Then she already opened the ice cream, and I really didn't want to eat it, so I just kept it on my cup holder right next to the AC. Then I fell asleep, and when I woke up, the ice cream completely melted and it went everywhere. So, I got a napkin and I tried to clean it. I was pretty panicked, but then the thing is when I'm panicking, I feel sleepy, so I slept again. And then when I woke up, I totally forgot about it, and we already reached, so I got up and left. We went back to the house.

And basically, everyone slept because they were kinda tired, and I did too. But while I was sleeping, I remembered about the ice cream, and I made a pact that after I got out, I would take it and throw it away, and then clean it later. But then when I woke up, they all said they wanted to go back to the temple or go to another temple because they felt like they came all the way here and then did nothing. But then this time, they'll take a lot of time, so they told me not to come. So, I had to stay at home, and I'm just like that's not bad. And then I realized that there's no Internet, and I immediately changed my mind. But then my aunt gave me her phone, so yeah, now it's fine.

They told me to just get ready and then wait for them to come back, so I was pretty much living life in that moment. I was playing games and stuff, and then I realized I have to get ready. They might come back soon, and I got dressed in under 10 minutes. Then, like 40 minutes passed by and I'm like, "Where are they?" So I texted my aunt, "Where are you?"

"What is going on?"

"Are you gonna come back soon?"

And they're like, "We're in the temple. Don't text me." And I felt pretty annoyed, so I just stopped and sat there. Then, an hour passed by and she finally texted me back. She's like, "Oh, we're coming in 15 minutes." And then 20 minutes went by and I'm like, "Where are you?" And then 10 minutes went by and I'm like, "You said 30 minutes. It's been two hours. Where are you?"

But then they just wouldn't admit anything.

"We reached."

I looked outside and they weren't anywhere to be seen. Another 10 minutes went by and they texted me saying they reached. That's when I finally heard some honking, and my mom opened the door. She was like, "Oh my gosh, I'm home." And I'm like, "FINALLY!"

I raced down and I forgot about my shoes. I'm like, "Aren't you all coming up?" And they shook their heads, so I went back up to put on my shoes. But then, while I was putting on my shoes, my mom asked, "Where is your aunt's phone?" And I replied, "I don't know. It's here somewhere." So I turned to the bedroom, but nothing was there. I was freaking out. How did I lose it? I literally looked everywhere, and I could not find it. I felt really sad. I'm just like, "Maybe my cousin took it." So I quickly put on my shoes and I went down and asked Ambadi, "Did you take your mom's phone?" And he's like, "Yeah, I did." And I'm like, "OK, fine. Case solved. It's closed." That's when I noticed this lady standing outside our car, and I just thought that it's probably some random neighbor. I got into the car, and 10 minutes went by. My mom is still not down. That's when I remembered my mom still thinks that my aunt's phone is lost. I know I should have gone up and told her that it was here, but I know my mom would come down anyway. So I just waited, and my gut feeling was right because eventually my mom came back and wasn't visibly mad. So I practically just won the lottery.

But when my mom got into the car, so did that random lady. Apparently, her name is Meera Aunty, one of her closest friends from college days who works in Thrissur as a Manager in Dhanalakshmi Bank.

So, like, I could totally tell that my sister was kinda mad because she didn't get to go to Munnar. We wanted to cheer her up, so Meera Aunty suggested going to the 'Sobha mall,' a famous mall in Thrissur district. She suggested that "Zudio" may have modern clothes of your taste. When we reached the entrance of Zudio, the security stopped us from entering the shop, saying that 'it is 9 PM, we are about to close." My sister and I couldn't believe our ears. In UAE, life starts after 9 PM, here it ends at 9 PM! Meera Aunty, who lived in almost all cities of Kerala, informed us that the one peculiarity she has noticed about Thrissur is that all the shops will close by 10 PM, and you rarely meet people on the road after this. After living in cities like Ernakulam and Trivandrum, she found it difficult to adjust here because of this. However, people here are nice and genuine, she added.

So, there we were, just sitting around, not sure what to do next. Finally, we were like, "Let's go grab something to eat!" But my sister is mad at everyone right now, so it was up to me to order food for both of us. No one else likes the same stuff we do, you know?

So, first, I thought, "McDonald's could be a good choice!" But then, when I got there, I couldn't find anything I really wanted.

Then I was like, "Pizza Hut it is!" But then, I realized that a whole pizza would be way too big for just the two of us. I mean, who can eat that much pizza? Not us!

So, I decided to skip my way over to this Thai restaurant. They had things like Momos and stuff. I wasn't in the mood for Momos. Did I ever mention I can be super indecisive sometimes?

And then I saw noodles, and finally, I came to the decision that I would eat noodles. So, I asked for some noodles, but I was pretty hesitant because I never ordered, and what if it was bad? Then all the blame would be on me, and I just wasted a bunch of money. But I'm like, it's fine, yeah, it's fine. So then, like, I rushed to my sister to ask her if noodles are fine.

But then each time she replied with "I don't care what you buy," and then when the food came, she stared at my face.

"You only bought one?" Like what do you want from me and it was exactly how I expected it to taste like. It wasn't that good and then I realized

'Oh my gosh I'm expecting too much of this cook cause not everyone can be that good of a cook as me "(I am just kidding I burn the kitchen down on a regular basis). Me and my sister barely finished it, but we didn't love it you know because it wasn't that great. It was slippery and spicy in the wrong ways. Left with no other choice, my sister finally decided to talk to me "go buy burger" and she gave me her money, so I didn't care and went to go buy a big mac.

In line there was this really pretty girl, so I just went up to her.

And said "you're really pretty."

And then she just stared at me and laughed like hello I give you a compliment, compliment me back and then she turned to me and whispers "you're pretty good looking too."

To me it sounded like such a backhanded compliment but like it's fine.

Eventually we ate the burgers and was good. On our way back, we dropped Meera Aunty near Thiruvampady Temple, where she parked her scooter.

When we reached home, my sister is like yeah you aren't sleeping on the bed because she slept on the ground last time. I had to sleep on the ground, and I honestly couldn't sleep at all and I don't know why but eventually somehow I slept so I guess that's fine.

DAY 14 – I DON'T DO NEEDLES!

So we woke up bright and early in the morning, like maybe 4:00 AM, because if we wanted to reach home by lunch, we would have to do that and my uncle had some important business to do, so we all had to wake up at the witching hour of 3 am and left.

The annoying thing is I got into the car half asleep, but when we started to drive, I just could not sleep. It was honestly annoying since I know I am sleep deprived, but my body won't sleep; so my reward is a good old headache.

So I tried to make conversation, but that was kinda boring, like pretty boring, and an hour went by so fast and then eventually two hours and by and then three. And since it was so early in the morning, we would reach our house faster because there was no one on the road, basically no traffic. But then around seven, there started to be more traffic, and that's when my uncle felt kinda sleepy. We decided that my uncle could just sleep in the car for some time so that we wouldn't potentially die in a car crash.

While we stopped, we found out that we stopped right next to a gents' salon, and we all really wanted to trim down cousin's hair because honestly, if he stood still for long enough, some bird would think that was his nest, that's how bad it was. So, my aunt, my mom, and my cousin went to have a haircut.

Now that everyone in the front is gone except my uncle, I realized that this is a perfect opportunity to sleep! I am not kidding when I tell you I haven't slept so easily in such a long time. I don't know for how long I slept, but when I woke up, everyone was like shaking me, and when I finally sat upright, I saw my cousin's hair. He got like a fade on the sides and then some hair on top, which was all curly. This is what I call a chummack boy haircut, but it was a hundred times better than his hair before.

And he was kind of worried that his teacher would shout at him, but honestly, the teacher has no right, because before he was a fire hazard. Once everyone got in and my mood to sleep was officially ruined, we continued driving back home. After like 3 hours, I started with my queries.

"How much longer?"

"Are we there yet?"

And each time, my uncle either didn't reply or said, "Five minutes."

After 4 '5 minutes,' we finally reached home, and I immediately got into my bed and started watching videos on my laptop. But obviously, I couldn't just sit there in peace for 5 minutes. My mom came up to me and said, "Go get dressed. We are going to the hospital."

Why? You might ask. This is because these days I have been feeling so weak and tired, and my mom has been forcing me to eat more food, but nothing is working. So my mom has been persistent to get me to go to the hospital, but we have been putting it off because we never had the time. However, the time has come, and we had to prioritize a visit to the hospital.

So, I got dressed and headed out by auto to the hospital known as 'Mother and Child Hospital' and fun fact, according to my mother, that's where I was born. So, I was pretty much expecting a lot from that hospital because if I was born there, it better be celebrating that I came back. But then when I went in, it wasn't much. It was like only two stories and was pretty old, like really old. But I should have expected that because my sister was also born here and it was my mom's childhood hospital, so it was probably 30 years old, give or take, and it wasn't that great.

We sat down to go to the gynecologist, and when we got in, I saw a really old lady sitting at the desk. When we went in, she immediately started asking me a bunch of questions. And when we were done, she was like, "You know, we should get a blood sample and check if you have thyroid or if something else is going on." And honestly, a blood sample is fine because I thought they were gonna prick my finger and then take some blood, and I was fine with that because it's just like a momentary type of pain. So, I went into the test lab in complete confidence. But turns out, they're gonna inject a needle into me, and I'm not okay with needles. I have beef with needles. No one likes needles.

So, I start overreacting, like moving around and repeating, "No, no, no." And all the nurses there got pretty angry and started shouting at me, "We have to go home." "We'll miss the bus." I'm like, "Okay, fine." So, I sat down, and my mom had to hold me down as they injected the needle into me. It didn't hurt that bad, but then eventually the pain kicked in because they had to literally tilt my arm and wait for blood to just flow out, and that took a lot of time. And it was pretty much like someone is stabbing you but slowly and watching all the life escape out of you. It's just sad. And when they took it out, I was basically hyperventilating because it hurt so bad.

They added that after one or two hours, if they test blood, they'll find out if I have iron deficiency or thyroid. I will get to know today in like 2 hours, and thyroid after 2 days. And honestly, after all the pain I went through, it better be either of the two because I do not want to suffer through more tests.

So, we had one or two hours to do anything we wanted. So, we walked around the block and started searching to see if there's anything interesting to do. But there was NOTHING, not even a cool-looking store. So, we went to this bakery, but then I didn't feel like eating. So, ultimately, we just went back into the hospital and sat in the waiting area.

Slowly but surely, more and more people started to leave. We were literally the only people left except for the staff. While I was at the hospital, I started reading the bulletin boards, and there was this sign that kind of confused me. So, I asked my mom what it meant. Apparently, in India, they're not allowed to find out the baby's gender before it's born. It's because there's a big deal about having boys in India, and not having a boy can bring shame to the family. Moreover, female foeticides are quite common. So, they made this rule to make sure people don't do something bad like getting rid of a baby if it's not a boy. You only find out if it's a boy or a girl after it's born. I actually think it's a pretty cool rule. It should be a thing everywhere, you know? After waiting for about 20 minutes and killing time by scrolling through my mom's phone, I went back to the lab. They handed me the test results, but I didn't bother reading them because I wasn't that interested. We picked up some medicine and headed home. It wasn't until we got back that my mom told me I had anemia. She didn't know much more about it because the doctor didn't talk about it much. They gave me some pills, but thankfully, there was also syrup, which was a relief since I hate taking pills. After I ate, I chowed down the pill easily, but the syrup was a different story—it tasted like metal, and I absolutely hated it. The whole day, I couldn't shake off that taste, and the worst part was that eating something else didn't help at all. So, I just hung out for the rest of the day, trying to make the most of it, and eventually crashed for the night.

DAY 15 – A NEW FRIEND

My mom used to complain about her body hurting all over, but I honestly didn't believe her. I mean, who has constant body pain and still has the energy to yell at everyone, right? It just didn't make sense to me. But then, when she came to India, she couldn't stop talking about going to an Ayurvedic hospital for a full-body massage. It became the center of everything she wanted to do. Even when we were in Thrissur, she'd say we couldn't do certain things because of her "Ayurvedic treatment." She even considered dyeing her hair, but then she'd be like, "What if the oil messes everything up?" So, it was one excuse after another, and it was honestly getting so tiring.

We were all curious to find out what this Ayurvedic treatment was about (well, basically only me), but I wasn't prepared for the fact that she'd end up being in the nude. Basically, my mom wanted someone to accompany her because she thought she'd be exhausted afterward. So, I had to tag along. We caught an auto, and it took us to a really secluded spot surrounded by greenery.

(And by greenery, I mean every single medicinal plant which they could grow there along with rubber plantation) and there was a cute little house on the side, which is used for inpatients who may come from faraway places.

When we got inside, a young lady greeted us. She looked like she was around 24, but later on, I found out she was actually 30 and already had a kid. But that didn't really matter. My mom went straight into a room, and there was no way I was going to be part of that scene. I mean, who wants to see their mom slathered in oil and naked? So, I happily stayed outside, choosing to remain blissfully ignorant.

The young lady seemed to find me interesting, and honestly, who wouldn't. At first, it was a bit awkward because I didn't know her, but then she introduced herself as Krishna Priya. And that was one of my sister's old friend's names and really close to my name. We started chatting, and surprisingly, we hit it off. Honestly, she was super cool, and I'm not just saying that 'cause I was bored. The surprising part was that she totally got why I didn't want to witness that whole "mom covered in oil" situation, something my mom didn't understand. Krishna Priya chechi was so laid-back, and we sort of connected. She asked me about my life, and I asked about hers.

I was curious about why she even worked there, and turns out, her life story was quite interesting. She had been learning Ayurvedic Medical Science to become a doctor for literally nine years, and now she is trying to write an exam to become an Ayurvedic doctor in Government, and honestly, I really wanted to just interview her. It sounded so cool to me, but I didn't want to play that card, you know? It all seemed a bit weird. Then, my mom started calling me out, getting annoyed that I wasn't up for witnessing the whole process. She's all like, "just watch this Ayurvedic treatment, blah blah." Yeah, okay, I get it, but still, I didn't sign up for this. Anyway, after some back and forth, I finally gave in and went in.

It was definitely strange seeing my mom in that state dipped in oil, but curiosity got the best of me, so I hung around to see what was going on. And let me tell you, it was pretty wild. They were warming up oil and throwing in leaves and stuff. This lady, Krishna Priya. She gave me the lowdown on everything they were doing. She even took me outside to show off their garden full of leaves and whatnot.

At one point, they got my mom in a sauna, but her head was sticking out like a turtle. I swear, it was hilarious.

Later, while we were going through pictures of her kid, I spotted these familiar tiles in the background of a video. I mentioned recognizing them, and she laughed it off like,

"Nah, you probably don't know."

But I was like, "Hold up, those are the tiles near Kavis Beauty Salon, right?"

And it turns out that she turns out to be some sort of distant relative. Her husband is connected to my family tree. I mean, she explained how, but honestly, it all went in one ear and out the other.

Honestly, this kind of scenario has always been a fear of mine – growing up, getting close to someone, and then bam, finding out we're long-lost cousins or something. It's just one of those things that could happen, you know? So, anyway, Ayurvedic treatment finally wrapped up, and we bounced. Gotta admit, it was seriously one of the coolest days ever. Getting to know Krishna Priya, getting the lowdown on those crazy treatments – it was mind-blowing.

On the auto ride back, my mom was practically running on fumes, so I had to get some warm water ready for her to clean up.

DAY 16 – AM I A DOCTOR NOW?

So, today I tagged along with my mom for her Ayurvedic treatment. I thought, why not lend a hand? While they were massaging her, they brought out a cloth sack filled with these sautéed Ayurvedic leaves. It looked like soup in a bag, seriously. They'd fry it up on a pan, check if it's not boiling lava hot, and then proceed to whack my mom with it. Oddly satisfying to watch. I ended up helping too, like frying the leaves before the whacking session. Am I on my way to becoming a doctor or what? They started teasing me, saying they only needed me around for that. But after a while, it got boring, and Krishna Priya chechi and I just quietly left.

I had this genius idea to check out the pharmacy section. While nosing around the medicines, I spotted a business card that said "Ayurvedic Health Center – US." And then it hit me – I could totally do a call-line thing with it. You know, like when you call a company and they're all like, "This is Pizza Hut, how can I help you?" I started wandering around, going all, "Ayurvedic Health Center, how can I assist you?" I was having a blast, but everyone else was visibly not impressed. I couldn't care less, though. I even filled my mom in on the fun.

Then, everyone seemed to gather around another room. Naturally, my curiosity led me there. My mom caught me up – apparently, there was a snake in the sauna. Or they thought so. They'd only seen the tail, but it was enough to freak everyone out. And then, out of nowhere, a lady strolls in, acting all casual, saying she just needs to check her BP. She whips out this BP monitor thingy, and it looked like a scale mixed with a thermometer. I'm like, "What even is that?" Turns out, you wait for it to keep increasing, and it eventually gives you your BP. Sounds sketchy to me, but hey, whatever floats their boat. Krishna Priya starts sharing the snake story with her, and she's like, "Oh, my brother's an exterminator. Let me check."

She gets a long stick and heads to the sauna with confidence. She opens the door with the stick, ready to whack the snake if it's there. But nothing. So then, they're like, "Maybe it slithered into the nearby bathroom?" They checked, My mom's freaked, thinking the snake's hiding somewhere and might spring a surprise bite on her. So, sauna plans are ditched, and they just use a soaked towel with hot medicinal water to rub her down instead.

"Our massager is this nice old aunty who's known our family for a long time. She's super chatty and loves to tell us scary stories. One day, she told us about something spooky that happened to her a while ago. She said that once, at noon, while she was sitting in the courtyard of the massage place (As I have already mentioned, it is located in a secluded place in the midst of rubber plantations) she spotted three mysterious shadows moving toward the nearby river exactly at 12 PM. According to her, these apparitions could either be ghosts or deities going to the river to take a bath.

Knowing that our dear friend Krishnapriya chechi often finds herself alone at the center, I quickly chimed in, suggesting that perhaps it was merely an optical illusion. To my surprise, my mother also nodded in agreement. When I squinted an eye on Aunty, I realized that she didn't like my intervention at all.

On the way back home, my mom showed me the river that massage aunty referred. It is 'Ithikkara river', locally known as 'Anappuzhaykal Aaru'. I was told that it is a 56 Km long river that originates from Kulathuppuzha, in the Western

Ghats. Ithikkara is a place nearby from which the river got its name. Locals are of the opinion that the word 'Ithikkara' has a strong connection with the legend 'Ithikkara Pakki', well known for his feats as a great robber and a friend of Kayamkulam Kochunni, the Robin Hood of Kerala. People say that he robbed only the richest people, informing them in advance and then distributed the treasure to the deserving families. Like a butterfly flitting from one flower to another, he moved swiftly and discreetly, leaving behind no trace of his presence. I guess every village has its own heroes and hundreds of local stories to share.

And after an eventful day, we headed back home. Around that time, my aunt shows up, and it clicks in my mom's brain that I was supposed to go check my test results for thyroid. My aunt had to come with me, so we hopped on her scooty. After waiting a bit, we finally got in, and the doctor walked in with some test files.

She drops the news that I don't have thyroid, but I'm at high risk. Okay, not exactly a party but not the end of the world. We asked about the anemia thing, 'cause I was clueless. Doc said my hemoglobin level is at 9, should be 12 to 14. So, yeah, I've got anemia, but not super severe. Solution? Chow down on iron-rich foods like red meat, pomegranate, fish – you know, that works. Slow and steady, my hemoglobin's gonna level up. Is it just me, or did anyone else freak a little when they heard "anemia"? School made it sound like such a big deal, but I've been feeling fine. And since it's not that extreme, I just got to mix up my food game a bit.

DAY 17 – BABY ME

Remember Krishna Priya chechi? Yeah, she lives super close to my place. So, I've been begging her for ages to let me visit her house. Every time I'd see her at the Ayurvedic clinic with my mom, I'd be like, "Today's the day I'm coming to your house!"

And I kept saying it on repeat. So, today she's like, "Yeah, you're coming over today."

I'm like, "Wait, what?"

So, she's all, "Around three, I'll swing by your place, and then we can head to mine. You can meet my kiddo."

I'm like, "Sure, sounds like a plan. Beats doing nothing."

Fast forward a bit – it's 3:00 PM, and my mom's friends are over again 'cause she's besties with half the universe. Eventually, the doorbell rings, and Krishna Priya chechi appears along with her husband and tiny tornado of a daughter. Adorable and full of energy, that one. The kid's like a whirlwind, goes around hugging everyone with her insane positivity. She spots a rocking chair and sits on it like a boss, not letting anyone else rock her. She's like, "Nah, I got this!" and she is basically exactly like me when I was young, I actually couldn't sit in one place for more than 30 seconds and she totally matched that energy.

Soon we decided to leave so we headed out and I walked in, only to be met by Krishna Priya's mother-in-law.

She's like, "Who's this? A new buddy for my daughter?"

I'm like, "Nah, not exactly. My mom used to go to the Ayurvedic place where Krishna chechi works, so I thought I'd check out her house."

All sorted. Krishna Priya chechi takes me upstairs, and the first thing that strikes me is how this place is like a maze. Twists, turns, unexpected surprises – I'm loving it. Up the stairs, there's a door to a laundry room (still under construction), and if you keep going up, there's a massive swing hanging from the ceiling. You can just chill there.

We step into her room, and it's Ariel central. Little miss tornado's all about The Little Mermaid and fish in general. She actually climbed up a cupboard and sat in it. She starts running out of steam, so her mother-in-law starts slicing up mangoes. The kid's playing around outside while we spot a stray cat that visits every day. The feline apparently comes over just to hang with her. Adorable, right? She's this animal lover – she even starts messing around with a worm she found. She's all, "Time to wake up, Mr. Worm!" She pokes it, and the thing actually responds. Who knew worms had alarm clocks?

Anyway, she's playing worm charades, and I'm munching on mango. Later, she's glued to YouTube on her iPad. But then, the internet decides it's had enough and won't connect to her iPad. So, Krishna Priya Chechi hands over her phone. While she's busy with tech support, I get the scoop on this cricket field across the road. Turns out, the land belonged to a guy with no kids, so his family divided it up, and now anybody can decide what to do with it. So, people just play cricket there.

As the day fades, I start feeling restless. I'm like, "I should head home." She's all like, "If you wanna go, you can go now." I'm thinking, "Cool, I'll just walk, it's literally a minute away." But nope, she's determined to drive me. So, we pile into the car, and I later find out her husband's a Marine engineer on a ship. Dude just got back from a trip and was probably dead tired. And there I am, bugging him to give me a lift. Guilt trip, much? Anyhow, we're chatting on the ride, talking about life in the UAE, CBSE stuff, and guess what? He finds out I'm the deputy head girl. Now that's some added pressure.

Finally, we get to a restaurant. They order tea, but I'm not a fan, so they go with lemonade. I could barely finish it, to be honest. It's actually pretty entertaining. Eventually, they drop me off at home. Weirdly, my sister's waiting for me. I'm like, "Aw, they care!" Turns out, the whole gang's gathered 'cause the internet's acting up. I'm thinking, "Wow, they really miss me." Turns out, they're just waiting for the internet fixer-upper to show up. After a while, he arrives, does his thing, he literally started to remove the entire main plug outlet and check the wires but he could find literally nothing wrong with the plug. Then came the grand reveal sometime around when my mom's friends came over my cousin probably turned off the main switch the whole time. So, we were just sitting there thinking the entire neighborhood was experiencing this. But nope it's just us. Yeah, classic move.

And that, folks, is how my day ended on a hilarious note.

DAY 18 – RECONNECTING WITH OLD FRIENDS

Remember a few days back, some of my mom's friends showed up. Guess what? Among the crowd was one of her old middle school buddies, Deena aunty. I used to be close with her daughter back when I was young, so that's the backstory. When Deena aunty swung by, my sis got all mad 'cause we hadn't done any shopping during our time in Thrissur. So, Deena aunty offered to take her shopping. It was all like, "Yeah, we're gonna hit the mall!" But truth be told, we didn't really think Deena aunty could make it work in her schedule. Surprise, surprise – she actually called up today and was like, "Let's go shopping, my daughter wants to go too."

The whole fam started getting ready. Then, Deena aunty messaged my mom. Turns out, she didn't have a car at the moment and was planning on hiring a taxi to get us to the mall. It sounded like a big hassle, and we were like, "Don't sweat it, don't come." But no, Deena aunty was already on the bus! So, it was decided that my uncle would play the chauffeur 'cause he didn't want to send us in a taxi. And moreover, Appuppan and Ammumma generously gave us pocket money for Onam shopping. We scrambled to get ready, and about 40 minutes later, Deena aunty rolled in. She'd been on a bus all this time! Major respect. We hopped in, with me stuck in the back with my cousin – not the comfiest spot.

Last time when we hit Lulu Mall, it took less than half an hour. This time, we're cruising like we're on a leisurely Sunday drive. And the worst part was that Deena aunty's daughter had tuition, so she'd circle back with her dad later. My excitement got a little deflated; the only reason why I came today was because I wanted to hang out with her.

As we're driving along, Deena aunty showed a shop that's all about boli and payasam. I'm not a fan of boli – like, who's into that? Apparently, my mom and everyone else are. So, the plan is to swing by there later. I was dreading it 'cause boli for dinner? Not my choice.

Time goes on, and we decide to hit up Jayalakshmi Silks so my mom can snag some outfits. She's got Onam celebrations in the pipeline, so she's gotta look the part. Meanwhile, I'm like, "Ugh, sitting around in a shop while they take forever to pick clothes? Really?" Anyway, we head into there, and it's like we're in a sardine can. Crowded as all heck. My mom's struggling to even see the clothes, so we decide it's a lost cause. We retreat and decide to explore another option – let's walk around and buy boli from the 'boli kada' (boli shop), as we have seen so many reels about this shop on Insta.

So, the gang's all in agreement, and I don't wanna be the party pooper, so I roll with it. We walk a good while and finally

reach our destination. It's like a fish market – everyone's shouting for what they want. We order up, I grab my food, and we call my uncle to let him know we're ready. I'm back in the car, clutching my boli in my hand.

Later, we decide to hit up another spot called Czarina, a famous designer boutique to visit their Onam collections. This time, my sis, my cousin, and I decide to opt out and stay in the car, chomping on boli. As my cousin takes the front seat, my sis slides into the back, and I'm stretched out in the last row. I'm like, "Yeah, time to feast on boli." Turns out, though, they stopped chowing down on boli altogether. So, here I am, digging into boli solo, and let me tell you, it's not great. My sister feels the same way, like, "Yeah, it's pretty bad." We all thought this place would be awesome 'cause of the long line and all, but popularity doesn't always translate to quality.

Then, I hear some knocking on the window, and I'm thinking, "Oh, they're back!" But no, it's Ponnuchechi, Deena's daughter. She looks the same as she did in 2019 – it's kinda wild. I'm psyched to see her, start asking questions, but she's a bit shy now, not too chatty. Eventually, Deena Aunty comes out, sees the gang inside, and calls everyone over. We gather up and head to Lulu Mall.

My Mom's on a shopping spree. The three of them end up snagging matching saris, which is actually pretty cute. We venture into Lulu and make a beeline for Westside to score some clothes. I told Ponnu Chechi I'm good at picking stuff out, and she's like, "I'm picky, though." I'm all confident – like, this is gonna be easy-peasy, right? Wrong.

We're in Westside, and the great outfit hunt begins. But wait, why isn't Deena Aunty's daughter, Ponnu chechi, picking anything? She's like, "Nah, nothing's interesting." I'm like, "Wait, what?" I ask her what kind of outfit she's looking for, *and she's like, "Something easy, casual, and not a lot of effort." I'm thinking, "Got it, I can find that."*

Here's where it takes a nosedive – I take on the challenge of helping her find something, and it's a total failure. Literally, every single item I point out is met with some kind of criticism – the color, the style, you name it. I'm like, "Okay, what colors do you like?" She's like, "Pink and black and white." Hold up, she's actually wearing black and white right now. I go into full-on advertising mode. Complimenting every dress like I'm in a marketing team. She's laughing, but I'm bummed.

Finally, we give up on Westside. My sis wants lipstick, so she goes to grab some while we wait. Then we decide to go upstairs and grab a bite at the mall's food court. We're trying to hit up a variety of spots for fun, but everyone's not exactly starving. We settle on ordering from Pizza Hut, but here's the twist – in UAE, there's this one pizza that everyone orders, the spicy Chicken Ranch pizza. But it's nowhere to be found in India, so we're like, "Let's try the Chicken Tikka pizza." Plus, some garlic bread. Food arrives, and I spot the differences between UAE Pizza Hut and the Indian version. Different plates, pizza cutter, the whole deal. Even the garlic bread's not the same – instead of the oval shape, it's like little loaves. Unexpected.

After munching down, we head downstairs and decide to head home. But wait, my uncle suddenly gets a hankering for food, so we U-turn and hit another town to grab some mutton and parotta. Odd choice, right? It's like, does Kerala only produce mutton? Turns out, it's his fave restaurant, so there we go. We drop them off, then head back home. Everyone's famished now, so we all munch on some parotta – except me, I'm chill. Finally, we crash and call it a day.

DAY 19 – INSECTS!

OK, I am not exaggerating when I tell you that insects are basically ruining my life. I'm not kidding! I know that there are considerably more insects in India than in the UAE, OK. I acknowledge the fact that I accept it. I embrace it, but I did not expect that at night a tiny praying mantis will nicely come to sip water from my water jug. Or when I go to turn off the light, a leaf-like insect is nicely sitting on it.

I did not expect for there to be a lizard on my toilet seat.

I seriously did not see any of this coming. I mean, who would've thought that insects would become such a huge deal for both me and my sister? It's like our never-ending battle against creepy crawlies, and honestly, it's a pretty big deal in our lives.

My sister, she's like, totally freaked out by lizards. Like, to the point where she won't even step into a bathroom unless she's absolutely sure it's lizard-free. And guess who gets to be her knight in shining armor? Yep, I am looking at her right here.

So, what happens is, she just pushes me right into the room or bathroom, and I have to be the fearless inspector. I mean, it's a tough job, but someone's gotta do it, right? I've got to check every nook and corner to make sure there are no lurking lizards waiting to surprise her.

Once I give the all-clear signal, she cautiously enters the bathroom, but here's the catch—I have to stand right outside, ready for action, just in case some lizard decides to make a surprise appearance in her face. It's kind of sad, but it's our insect-inhabited reality.

And let me tell you, insects are like, everywhere here. I mean, you can't escape them. They're like these tiny, sneaky ninjas, always ready to pop up when you least expect it. It's like we're in a never-ending battle against these little critters, and we've become quite the bug experts in the process.

Oh, my goodness, let me tell you about the great Indian noodle adventure! So, a few days back, I asked my aunt to grab some noodles from the store, and she did. But here's the thing about Indian noodles – they come in this big plastic bag, not individually wrapped like they should be.

So, picture this: I open one noodle packet, take out a handful, and suddenly, it's like a bug magnet! Bugs start showing up everywhere, like they're on a mission to join the noodle party. Who wants to eat noodles with extra protein, right? They're even chilling on the packet cover and hiding in the noodle crevices.

When it is cooking time. Ants are everywhere in the kitchen, and I'm like, "Sister, we got a bug situation!" But she's all like, "Oh, one or two ants are fine, no big deal." So I whip up her noodles, and guess what? She loves it! She's like, "These noodles are better than your usual, maybe the ants added some secret flavor."

But then, the second time she asked me to cook noodles, she saw the ant army floating in the water, and she was like, "Yeah, no thanks, I don't need."

But wait, there's more! At night, when I'm busy working on my top-secret book (well, not that secret), these fireflies decide to crash my party. One zooms into my room, and I'm panicking because, honestly, I have no clue why I'm scared of a firefly, but I am!

I can't even see it properly because it's playing hide and seek behind me. What if I accidentally squash it, and it's mad at me? These insects are obsessed with my laptop. They're like, "Ooh, shiny!" and keep bumping into it. One time a cockroach jumped on me and I fling flicked it off and then it came again and started crawling up my hand, and I couldn't see it properly as it was so dark. Oh my gosh! It was terrible, you know.

Because of all these, I've got a serious hate-hate relationship with insects. They're just too much and literally have no business other than being so annoying. They can climb walls, so why are they also trying to take over the floor as well? It's like they can't decide whether they want to be Spider-Man or the King of the Ground.

These insects are like the unofficial rulers of my life here, and I miss my dad and the UAE.

DAY 20 – THE GRAND FINALE

I gotta spill the beans here – leaving India is hitting me harder than a ton of bricks. I know it might sound like I'm being all dramatic, but I'm laying it straight – I'm seriously bummed out. Let me lay out why this whole leaving thing is depressing:

So, once I touch down in the UAE, I'm like slammed with a whole bunch of stuff to do – holiday homework, finishing up paintings, wrapping up some books. But back in India, I'm just kicking back, chilling, and strolling out every single day like it am not into big things.

There's this funky dynamic with my extended family. Every day's like a surprise packet of who knows what. It's like, they're discovering my quirks and I'm catching them in all their quirky glory. It's basically a non-stop entertainment show, and I'm gonna miss that big time.

And then, there's the classic cousin bickering. At home, me and my sister barely cross paths – she's either glued to her tuition or hanging out with pals or complaining about back pain (which is my mom's jam too, oddly). So, in India, it's like a reunion of sorts, but now that's all hitting the brakes.

But here's the scoop – none of this even matters right now 'cause today's the curtain call. And let me tell you, this last day? It's been like a rollercoaster ride, like a grand finale in a blockbuster movie.

My sister has got a thing for organizing stuff – she's practically a wizard when it comes to that. This morning, she goes all Mary Poppins on my suitcase, folding my clothes like they're origami masterpieces. Why?? You might ask that's because my sister is obsessed with keeping everything clean even my things so when she saw my suitcase plopped up in a mess she could not handle it and most of her clothes are trapped in my suitcase too. So I got a free cleanout while she went through all my clothes, and this was an amazing sight and my entire family came to watch her work her magic.

Later in the evening, my mom was all strict about hitting up the temple. Because our last temple visit was an utter flop, so she was determined to turn things around. Cue the auto rickshaw call – me, my sister, my mom, and my cousin Ambadi all hopped in for what was shaping up to be quite the adventure.

We hit maybe four temples, starting with this one I oddly recognized. Don't ask me how. Good vibes. Here's the thing– I was running late, typical me, fumbling with my shoes and whatnot.

My mom's all, "Hey, we are running late either way you can't wear your shoes to the temple don't bother wearing them."

So, like a good obedient daughter, I didn't wear any.

And off we went shoeless into the temple. Surprisingly, no shoe-removing rituals, a win in my book.

Into the temple we went, prayer vibes and all. Now, here's my confession: every time I start my prayers, it's like I'm rattling off a laundry list of things I wanna achieve in the year. I swear, it's like I'm spitting bars in there. But hey, that's just me. While I'm in this prayer rap, my fam's already trotting off to the next spot. Yeah, embarrassing much?

So, auto mode again, and we're off to this cave-like temple. As we step out, it's that perfect time when the sun's dipping and the sky's putting on a show. Clouds, mountains.. My sis suddenly points at something, all like, "Wait, isn't that Jatayu Para?" (I forgot to tell you, the famous Jatayu Rock is located nearby our place)

My mom's quick with a, "Nah, Jatayu Para's the other way."

But me? I'm convinced – I spot this god-like shape in the clouds, and I'm like, "Nah, it's over there."

We even consulted the auto rickshaw dude, who's like,

"Nah, you're off." Total optical illusion, those clouds were playing tricks on us. How dare they.

Anyway, we get to this temple that's carved right out of rock, First off, this temple is like a total rock star – literally! The temple is carved out of a massive rock face and features intricate rock-cut architecture and it's super old, like from the 6th and 8th century CE, during the reign of the Pandya dynasty.. Can you believe that? It's dedicated to Lord Shiva and is filled with super cool sculptures.

Now, speaking of sculptures, they're like the rock stars of the temple. There are carvings of all sorts of Hindu gods and goddesses, and even some mythological scenes.

Chummadu Para

People have been coming here for ages to worship and get blessings from Lord Shiva. But for me, it was like stepping into a time machine and seeing what life was like way back when. And on the flip side, there's this elephant carving you could even spot the trunk! What surprised me the most apparently it took 13 years to carve this place out of rock. I mean, my apartment building with its 25 floors took less than a year, and don't even get me started on the Burj Khalifa, the tallest building in the world two years tops! Hey! I realize, they didn't have fancy machines back then, People relied on their hands and their sheer determination to carve this awesome temple out of a rock. A great job indeed and they need a BIG ROUND OF APPLAUSE.

According to locals, this rock was brought here by the incarnations of Lord Shiva, including Nandi. We spotted another small rock here as well. Locals call it 'chummadu para', as it is believed to be used to support and relieve pain when a bigger rock is kept on the head.

I want to say that this place is not just a temple; it's like a history lesson carved in stone. The ancient artisans who worked on these sculptures must have been total pros. And you can see the dedication in every detail.

Locals also believe that the Pandavas visited this place during their exile. It may be true, as the Jadayu rock is located just 10 km away from here. Jadayu rock isn't just a geological wonder; it holds a legendary tale that has been passed down through generations.

The story goes back to the age of epic heroes and mythical adventures, to the great Indian epic, the Ramayana. In the Ramayana, there's a character named Jatayu, a majestic eagle-like bird known as a "Garuda." Jatayu was no ordinary bird; he was the son of Aruna, the charioteer of the sun god Surya.

Now, Jatayu was a noble and valiant bird, and he had a pivotal role to play in the grand saga of Lord Rama's quest to rescue his beloved wife, Sita, from the demon king Ravana.

One fateful day, as Ravana was carrying Sita away to his kingdom of Lanka, Jatayu, with his keen eyes and heroic heart, spotted the abduction. He couldn't stand idly by while a helpless woman was taken against her will. With all his might, Jatayu swooped down to rescue Sita and engaged in a fierce battle with Ravana.

Their epic battle raged on, with Jatayu displaying incredible courage and valor. But Ravana, being a formidable adversary, ultimately overpowered the brave bird. Jatayu was gravely wounded, and as he lay on the ground, he managed to convey to Lord Rama and his brother, Lord Lakshmana, the direction in which Ravana had taken Sita.

Jatayu's sacrifice and unwavering determination to protect Sita touched the hearts of Lord Rama and Lakshmana. They revered him as a noble friend and a true hero. Jatayu's valiant act became a symbol of selflessness and courage.

As the years passed, the place where Jatayu fought his last battle and sacrificed his life came to be known as Jatayu Rock. It's believed that the massive rock formation resembles the outstretched wings of Jatayu, perpetually guarding the memory of his heroic sacrifice. Recently, it has been converted into JADAYU EARTH CENTRE. A giant concrete statue of Jadayu was sculpted by Rajiv Anchal over 10 years. It spreads over 65 acres of multi-terrain landscape of caves, hills, and valleys. The statue is 200 feet long, 150 feet wide, and 70 feet high, making it the largest functional bird sculpture in the world.

The sculpture always caught my attention whenever I pass through that area.

I assure you that a trip to Jadayu Sculpture and Kottukkal Rock Temple will be an adventure into history and art. If you ever get the chance to go, don't miss it! It's like a journey through time, and you'll come back with a gazillion stories to tell.

Speaking about this, I remember another curious thing. Whenever we pass through Chadayamangalam – Kottukkal by route, we always go through a place called 'Kalladathani'. Our driver Vijayan Uncle, who is a good storyteller, points out to a rubber plantation and says "Look, Sayippinte thottam" (Plantation belongs to a British National). I never knew that foreign nationals could own property in India. I was told that when the British left India after independence, most of them sold off their properties and fled, but this particular person was so fond of this place and decided to keep the property. I was informed that he used to visit this plantation and stays in the attached farmhouse at least once a year, and his precedents continue that practice, and they even keep good communication with the locals there. Once there was a labor dispute in that plantation, and even the British embassy diplomats directly came over there for negotiations as it belonged to their national. I am not sure whether all this information is true, as it is a word of mouth.

Moving on, we hit up another temple, but it's playing hard to get. After that, we're near my mom's aunt's place, and my cousin's like, "Hey, let's walk there."

But as you might recall, I am NOT wearing shoes, so I am walking on the road, getting poked left and right by pointy stuff. My cousin's got the wrong house! And started asking her about her supposed granddaughter who lived here even though she didn't have one.

When we were going back to the auto rickshaw, my mom's feeling guilty for my shoeless struggle and offers up her shoes. But I know better – she'd be complaining about sore feet soon enough. So, no dice. Then, we're en route to a final temple, but guess what? There was no light, so when we spot a man over there, we asked him about the temple and apparently it's closed, which was totally not fair. It was supposed to close at 7.30 PM, but they decided to close 10 minutes earlier. So sad!

Then we headed back home.

And that's a wrap on the temple tour.

We snagged the package, and I was eyeballing all those skincare treasures like they were pure gold. My sis and my aunt were having this silent battle of jealousy, while I'm like, "You guys, I want in on this haul too!"

The airport shuffle to the UAE is a whole different vibe. We're boarding the flight, and surprise, I actually catch some Z's this time. I was out cold, dreaming of all the adventures ahead. Suddenly, I'm waking up, and we're landing. I'm like, "Wait, when did the food even come?" The sleep was that good.

We're back in the car, and it's like watching a tennis match between my mom and my dad. They're exchanging words, and I'm just sitting there thinking, "Welcome to the family reunion, right?"

Back on home turf, it's like a warm embrace from an old friend. Reuniting with the landscape, the streets, and my room – it's all a blast of comfort. I took a shower that felt like it lasted for ages, soaking in every drop of water. But then, there's the dust on the floor, and I'm thinking, "Seriously, who invited you?" So, I grabbed a mop and got down to business.

Finally, the day winds down with my dad showing up from the office. Looking back, it was like the perfect ending to a wild chapter. The crazy experiences, the rollercoaster of emotions, and the moments that just stuck – they all add up to this epic final chapter.

www.ingramcontent.com/pod-product-compliance
Lightning Source LLC
LaVergne TN
LVHW021252160826
845679LV00001B/54

9798891862609